Play Grounds

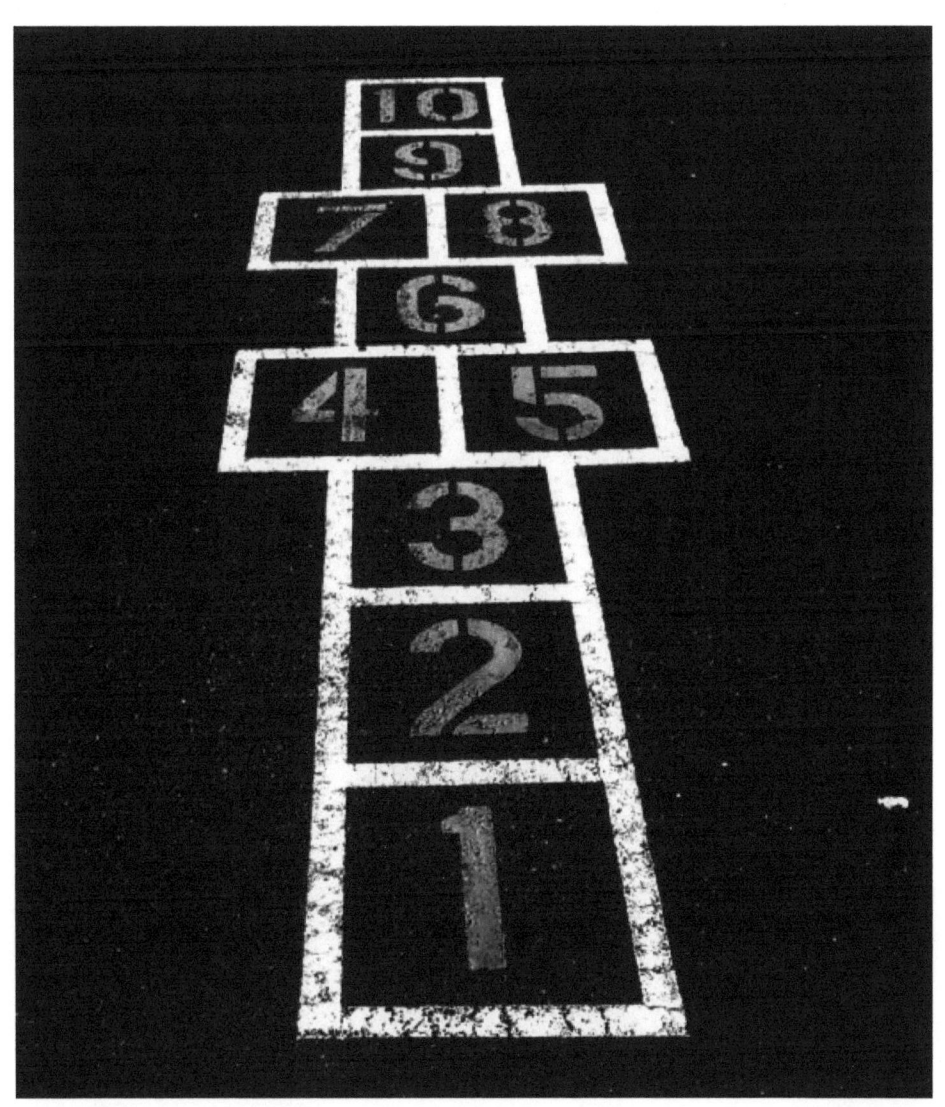

How Vision Is Learned by Children
by Jerry Newman

4 Quarters Technology, LLC
141 N. Pleasant Street
Amherst, Massachusetts
01004

First Edition

For my Dad

Vision is given to us by nature and learned by us from our surroundings.

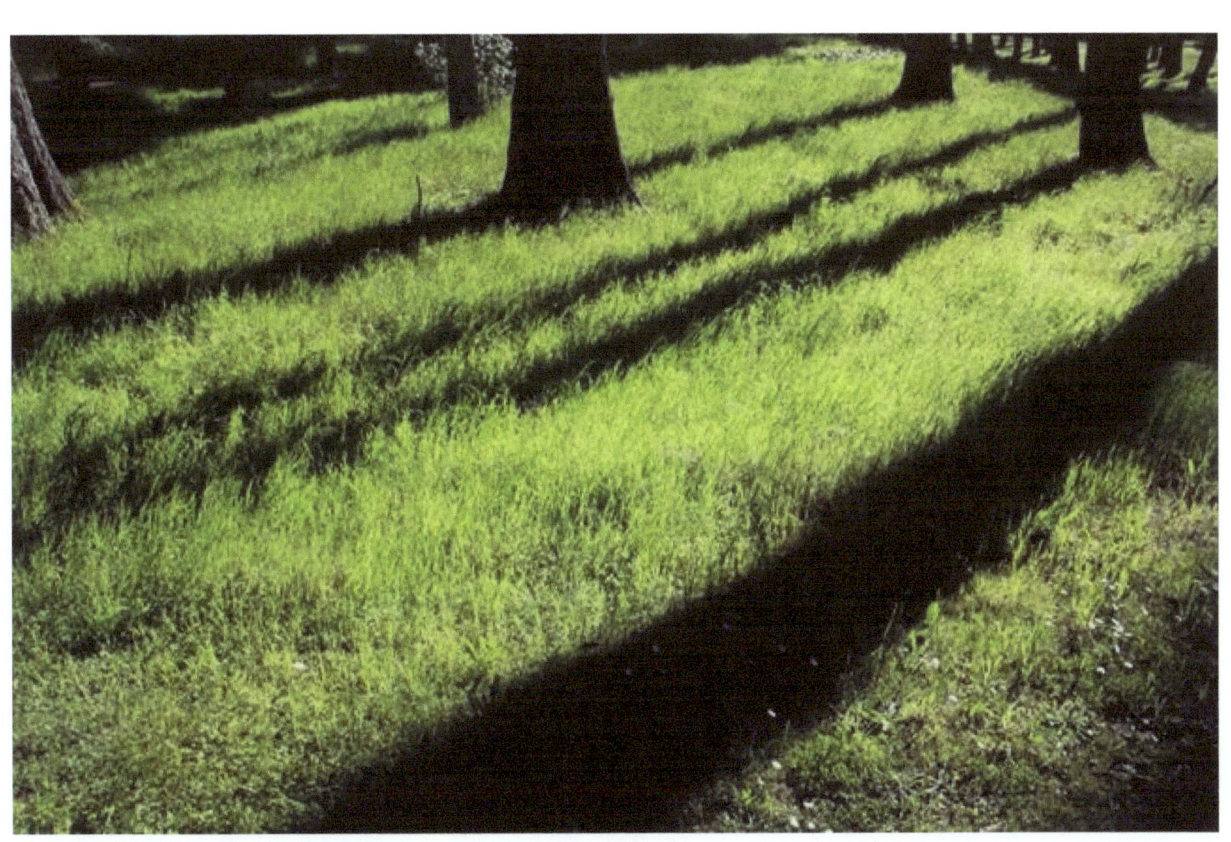

We start by seeing our parents around the house;
we focus and we stand up to see the world.

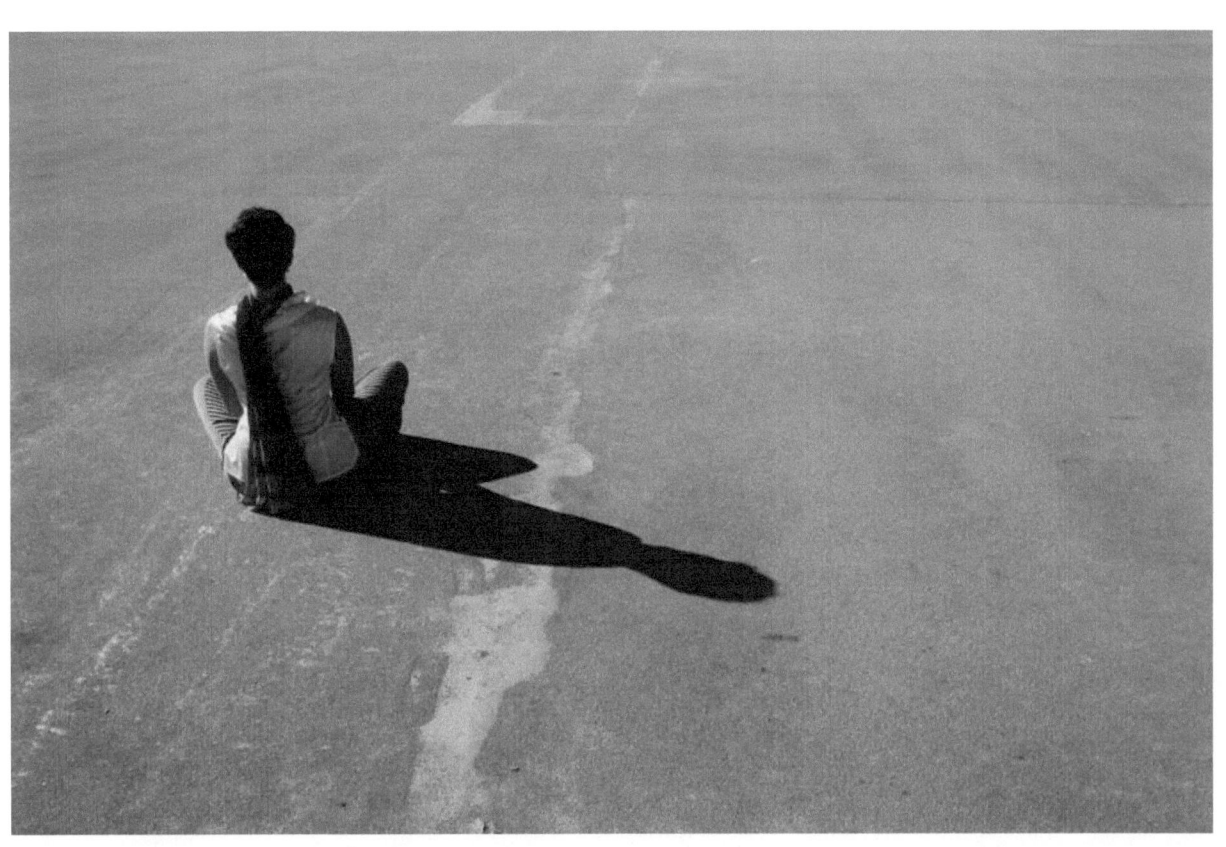

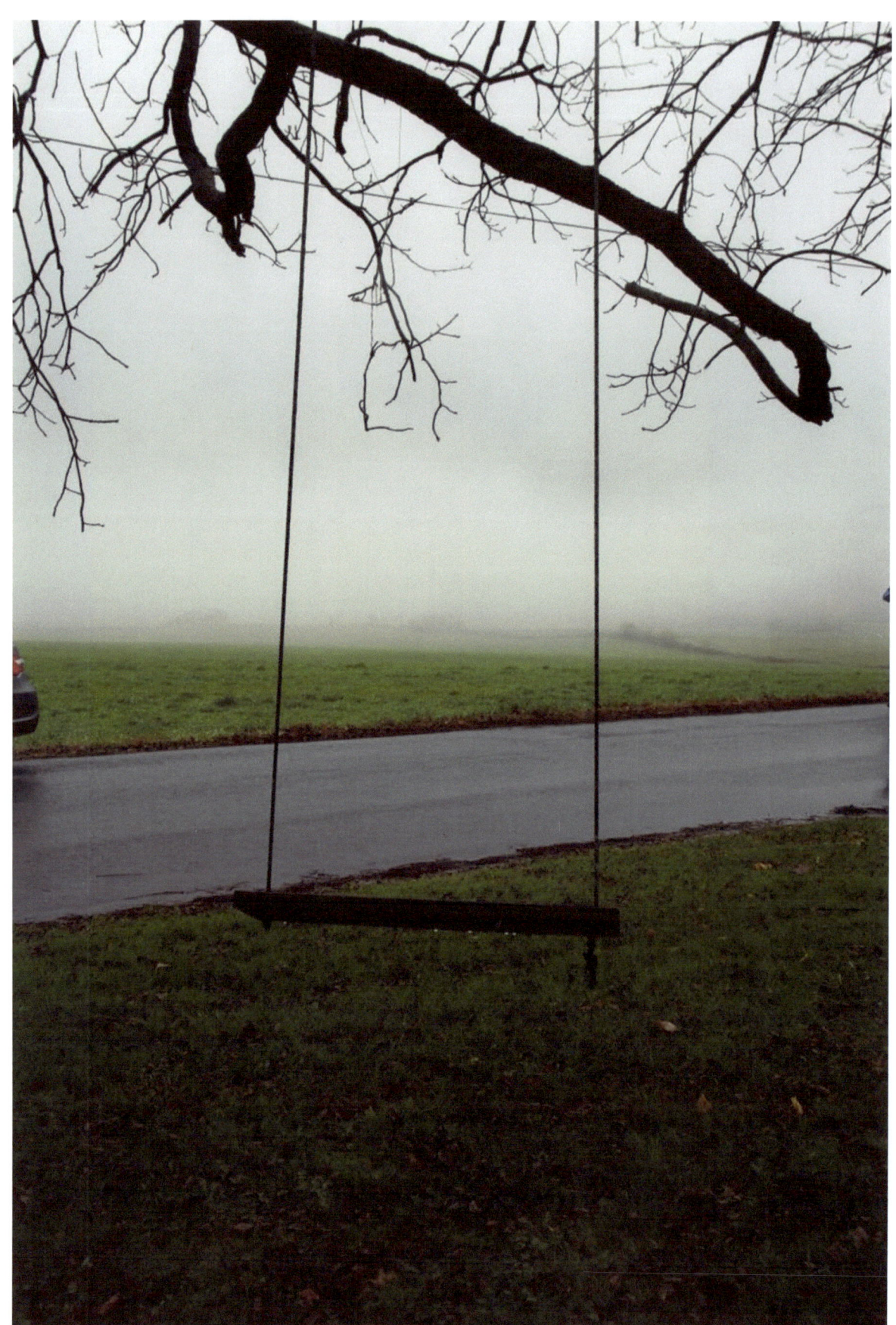

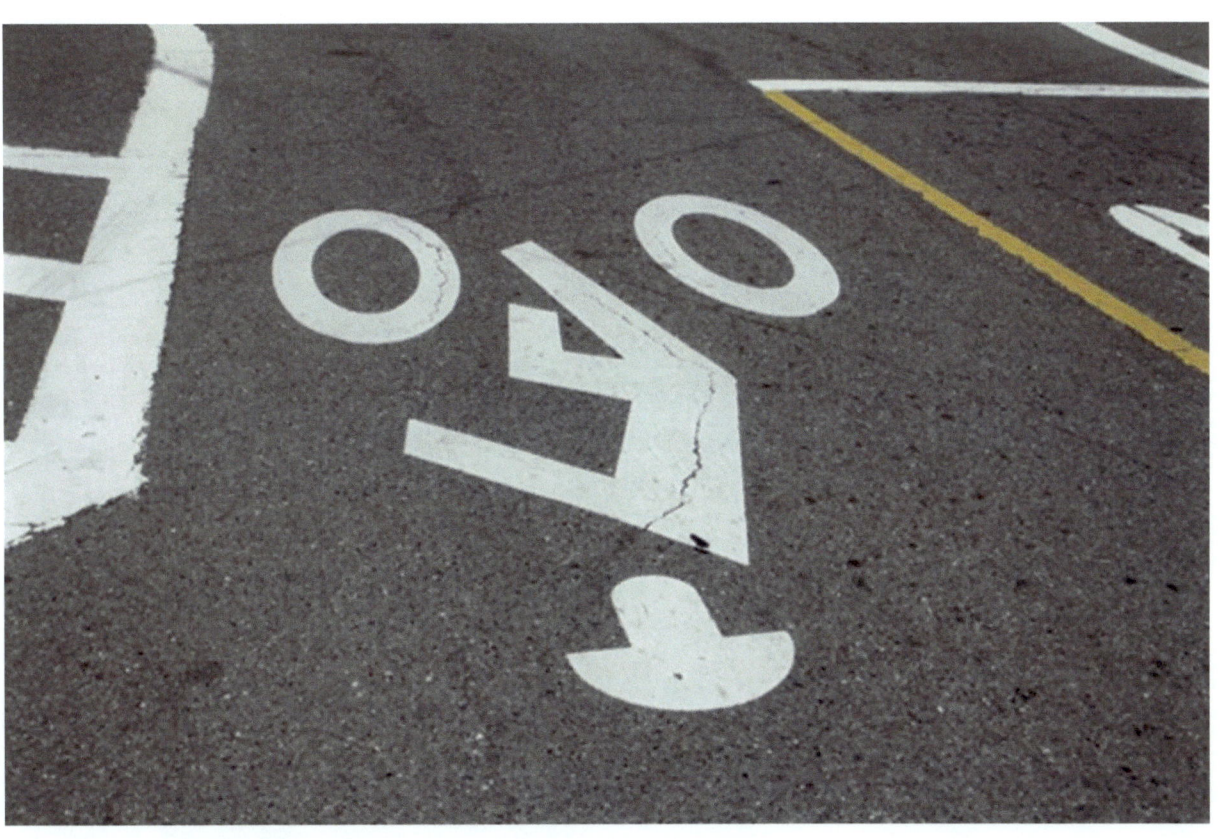

The world is shown to us by
our parents:
These are your feet.
These are shoes.

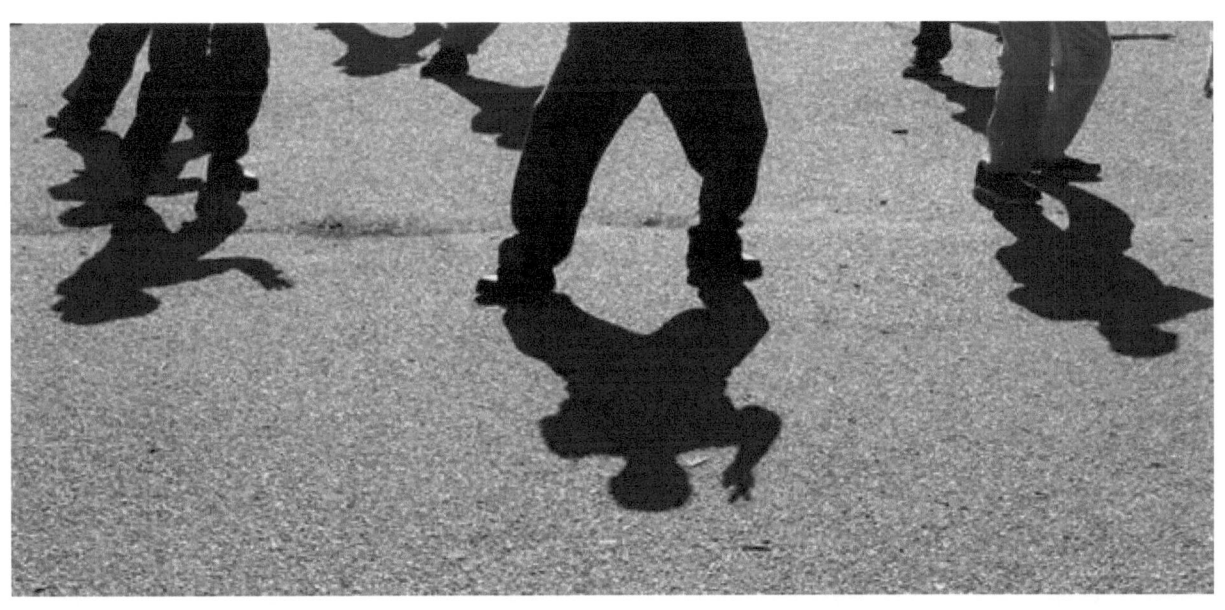

As we get older,
slowly we absorb more places and other people
placed before our eyes.

We are "acculturated."

We are starting to see what others show us.
The great divide occurs when we go off to
school.

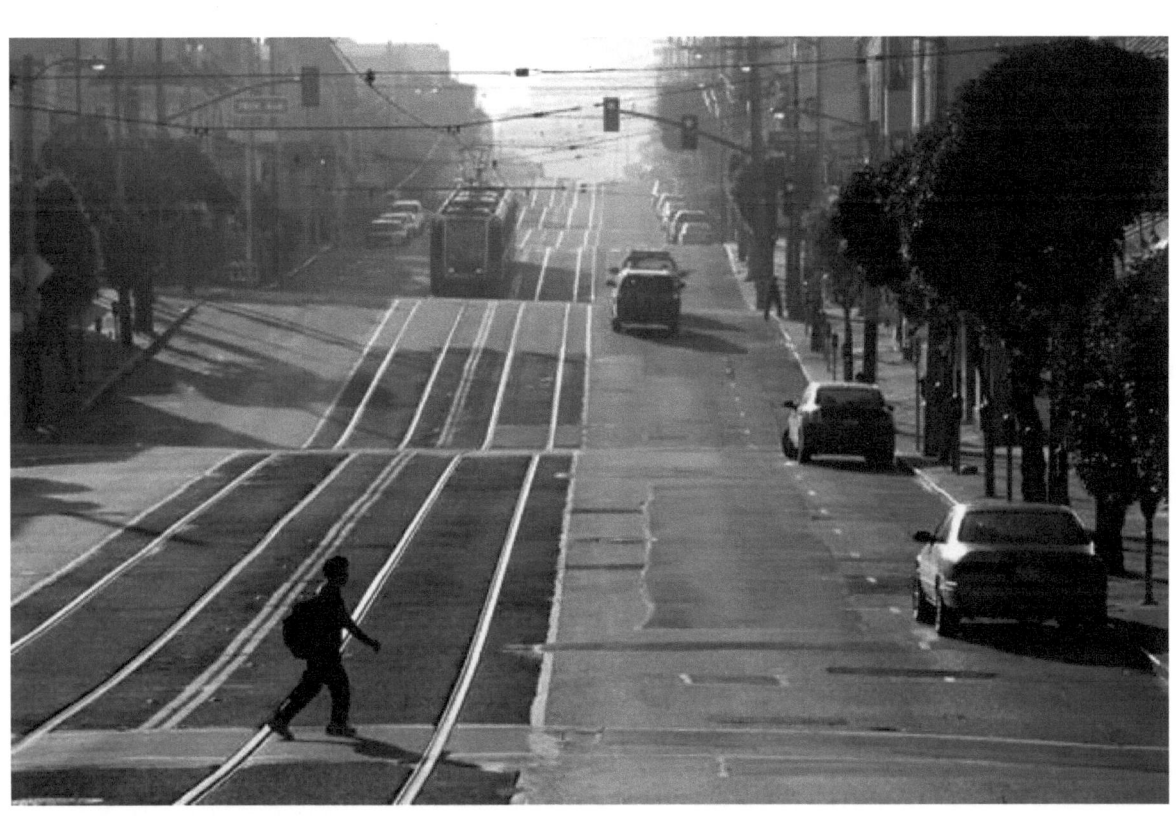

We see others and we see what the culture wants us to see.

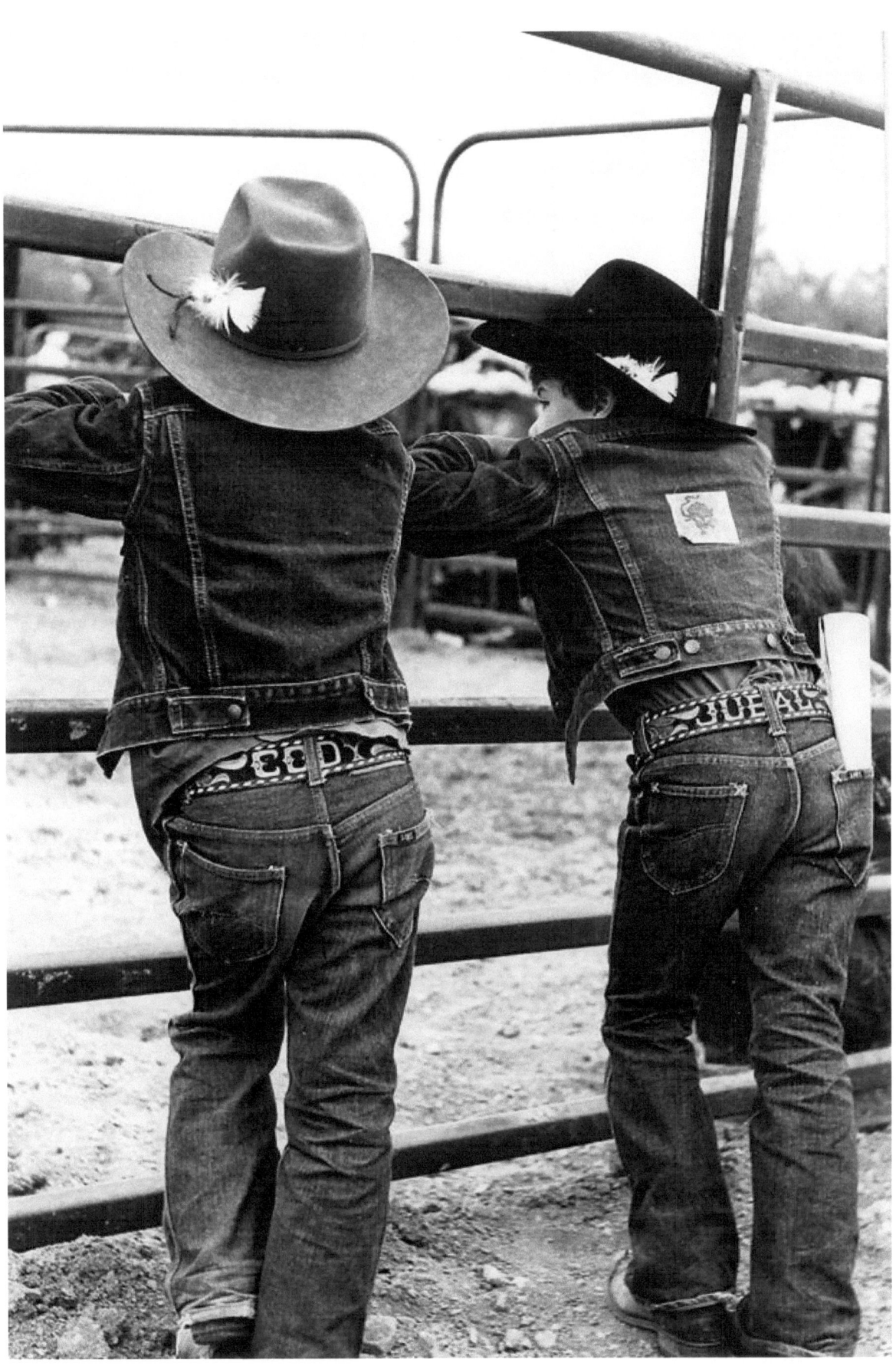

We need a Story.
We now desire a series of pictures in our head.
We look for a Conclusion.
And the process starts again.

Some art is static, like a still photograph.
Why more?
Acculturation: the ability of society to interact
with individual members of society at the most basic
level.
Pictures, sounds stories, attitudes.

Our brain never stops seeing everything,
school all of the time.

We want video, we want audio accompaniment.
We want a story, again. We want to remember some
stories, so we see and hear the story over and over
again.

We want to imprint the story and interact with our
consciousness.
We want to form behavior.
So we start a picture, a word, or a flash of sight.
Does acculturation help, or does it hinder?

You tell me.

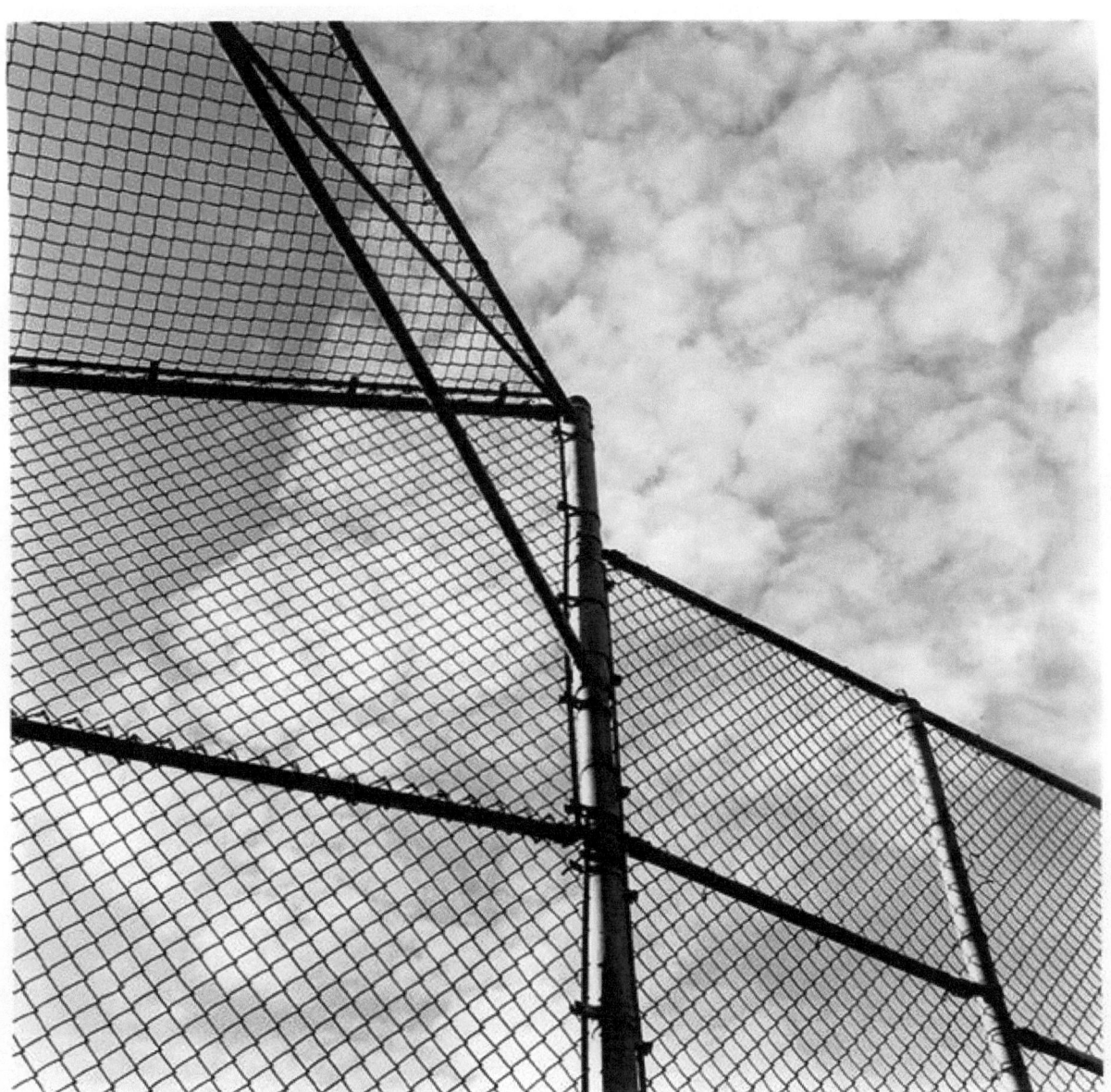

We see lines.

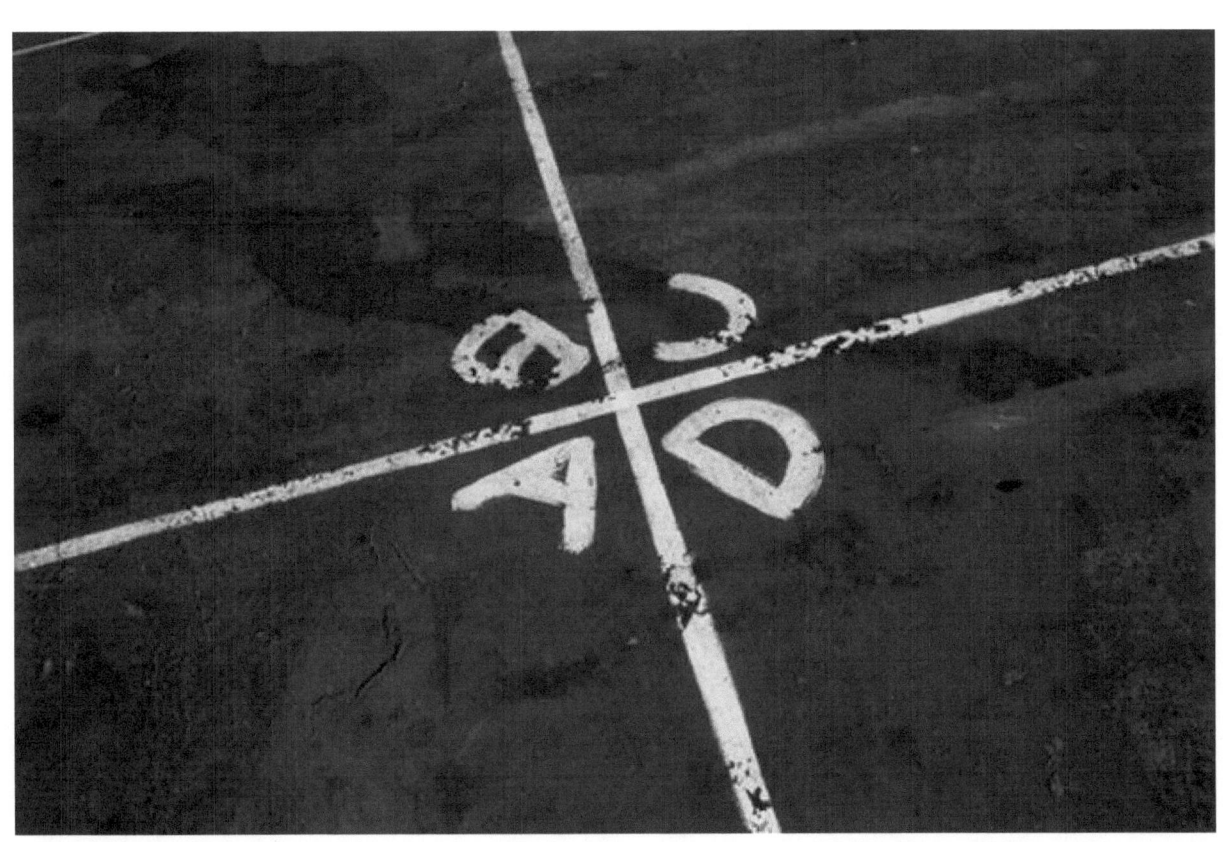

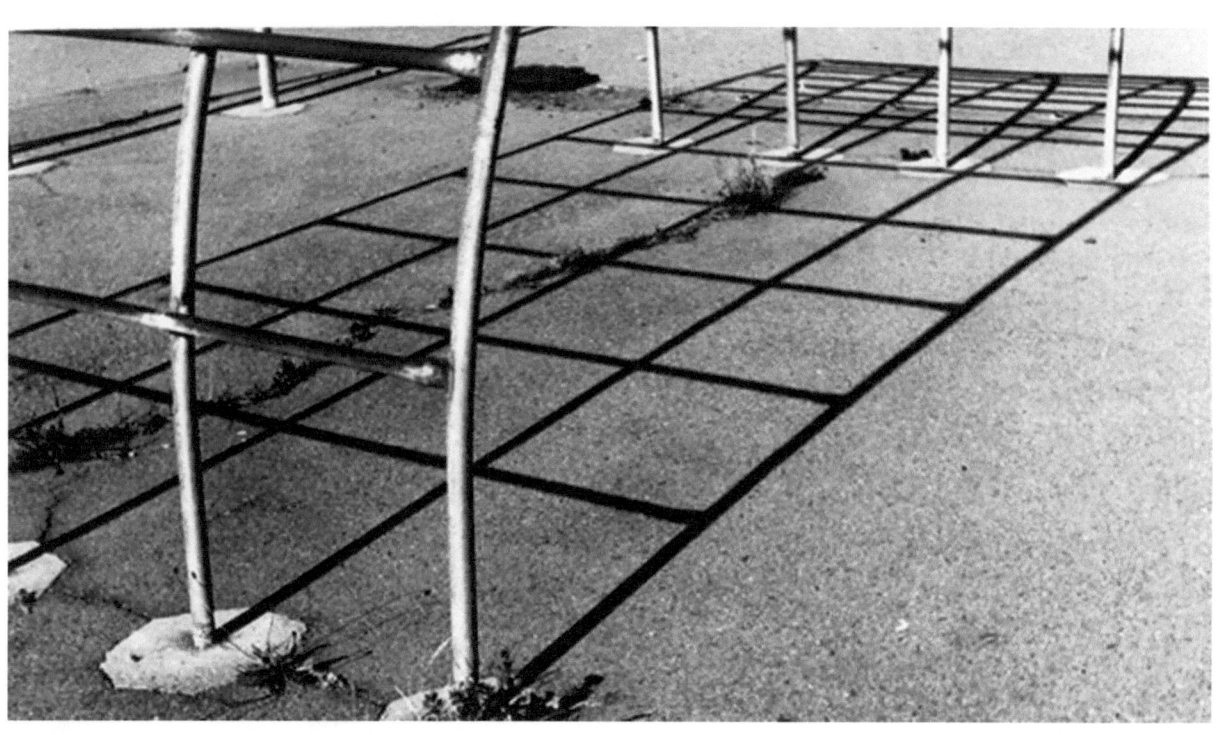

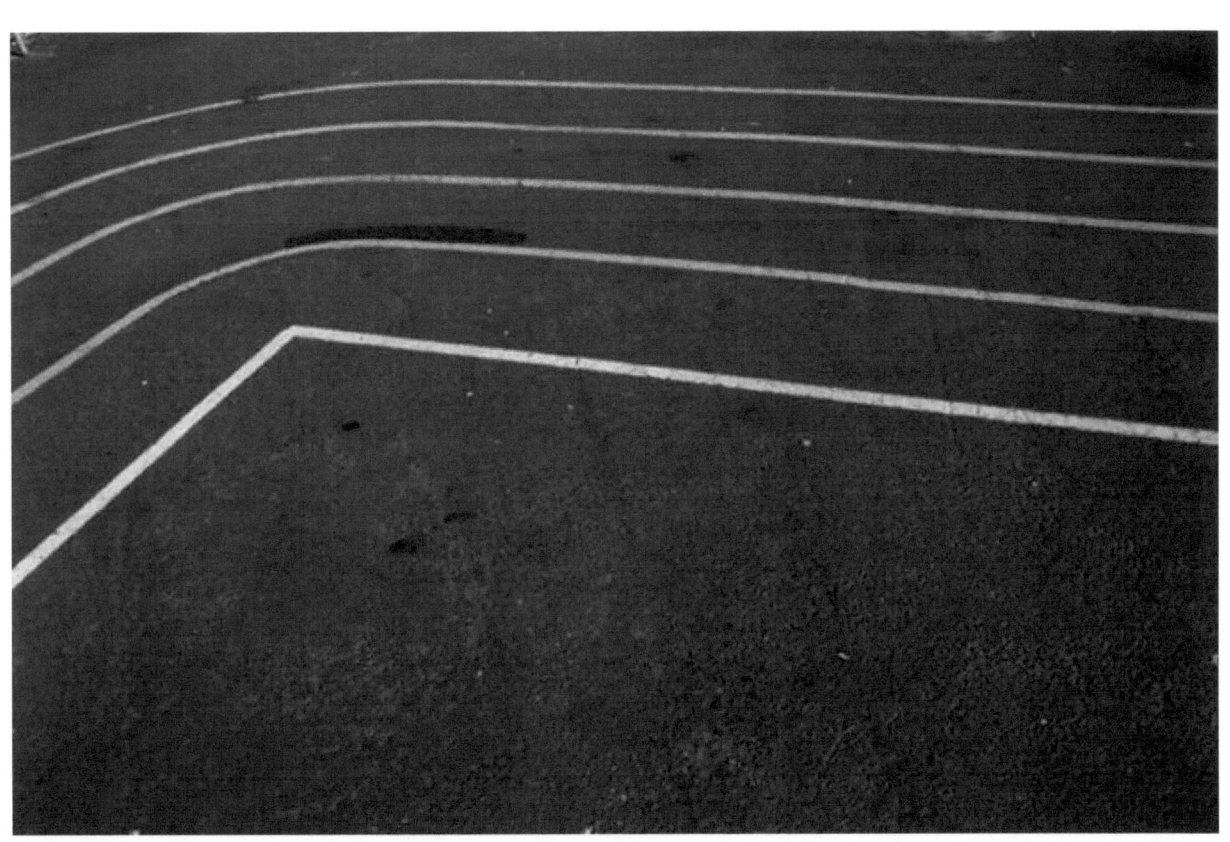

We see circles.

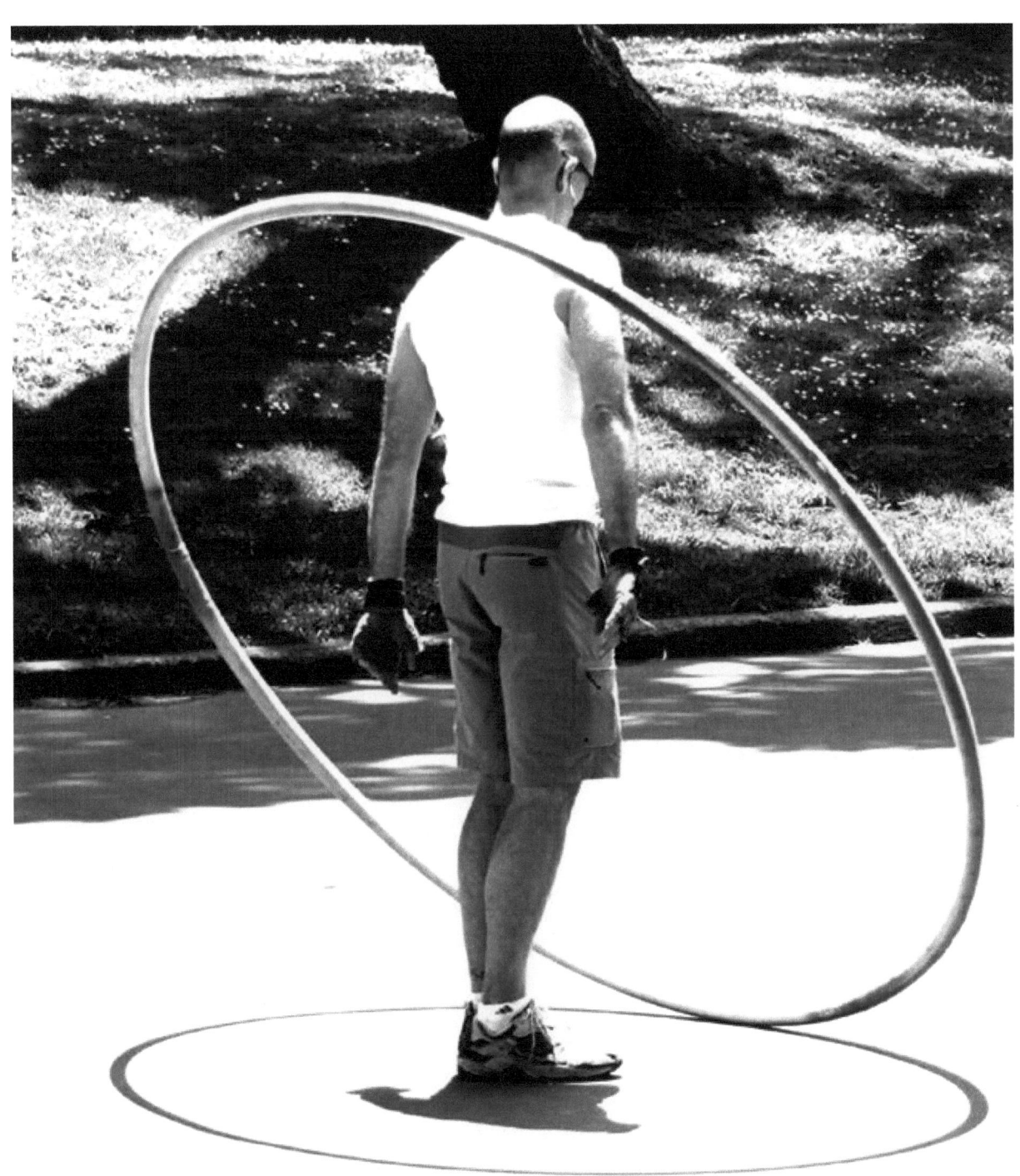

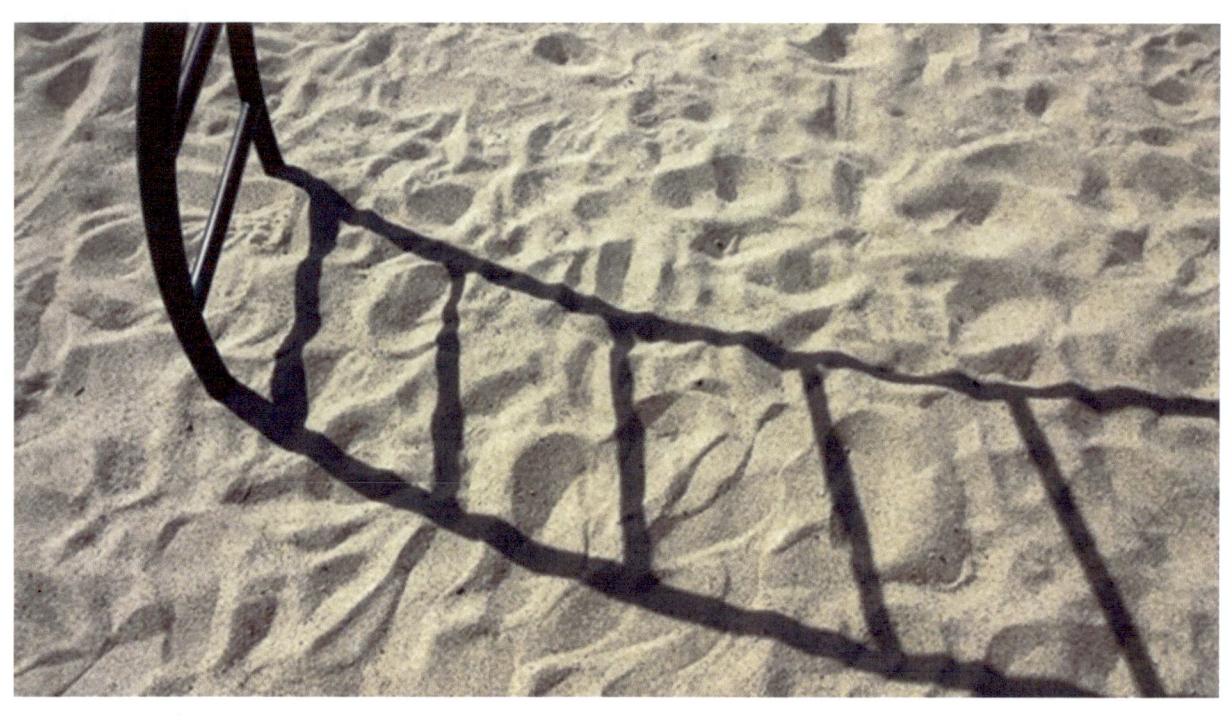

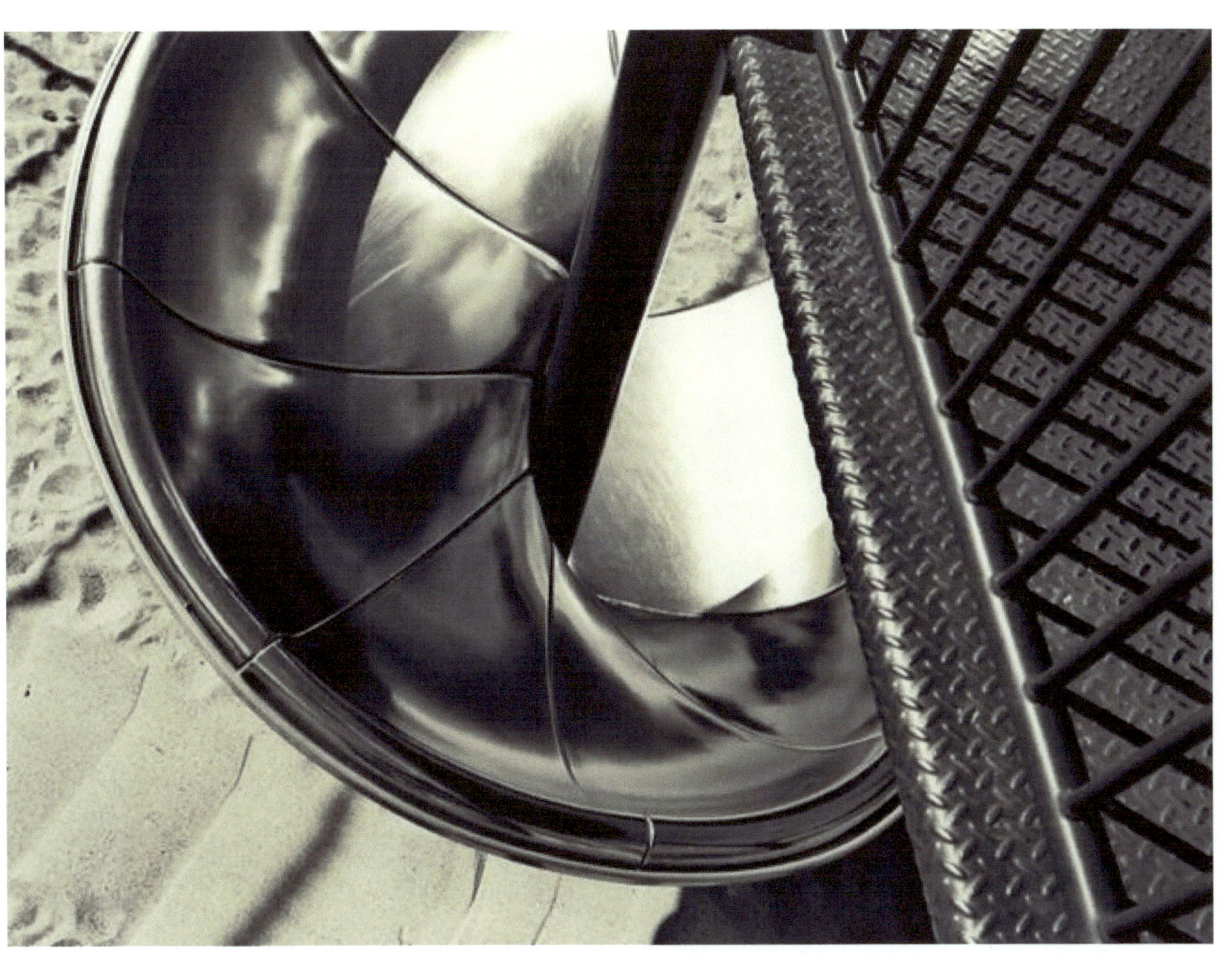

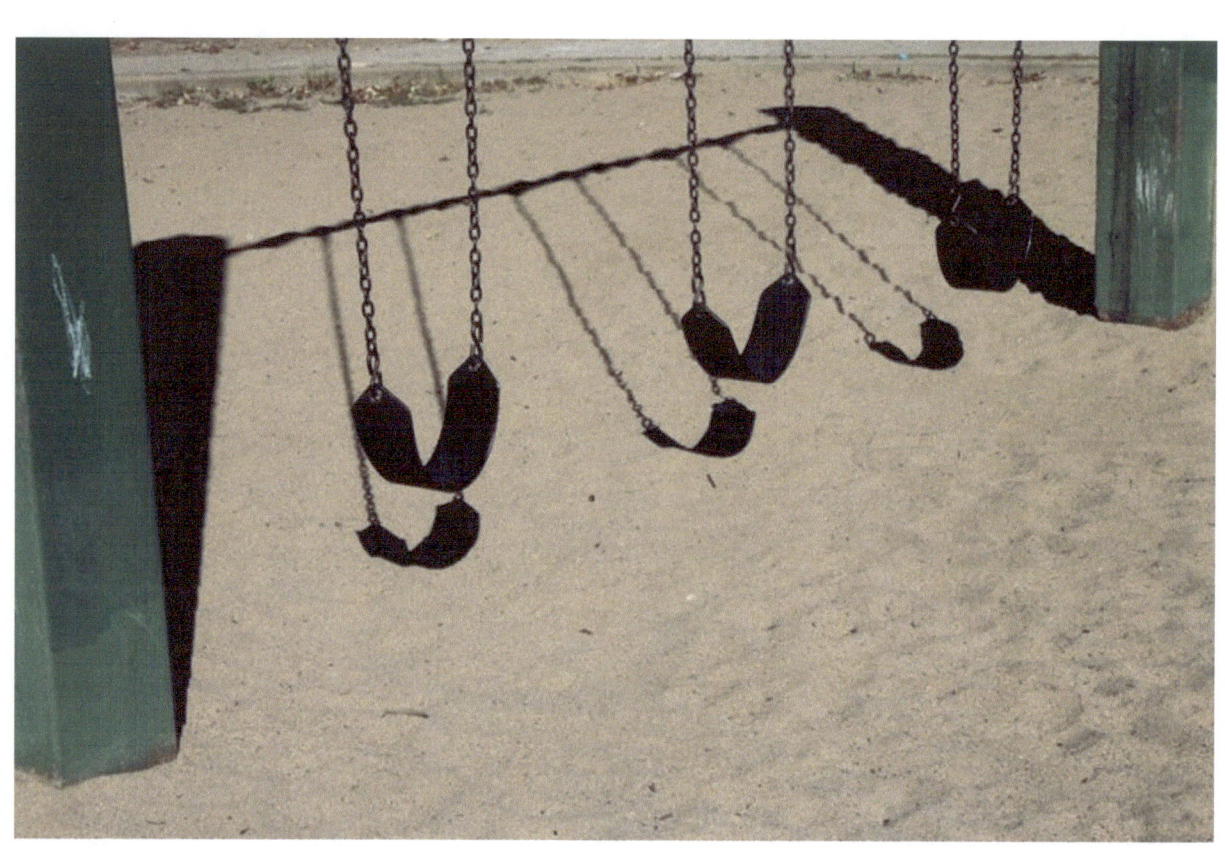

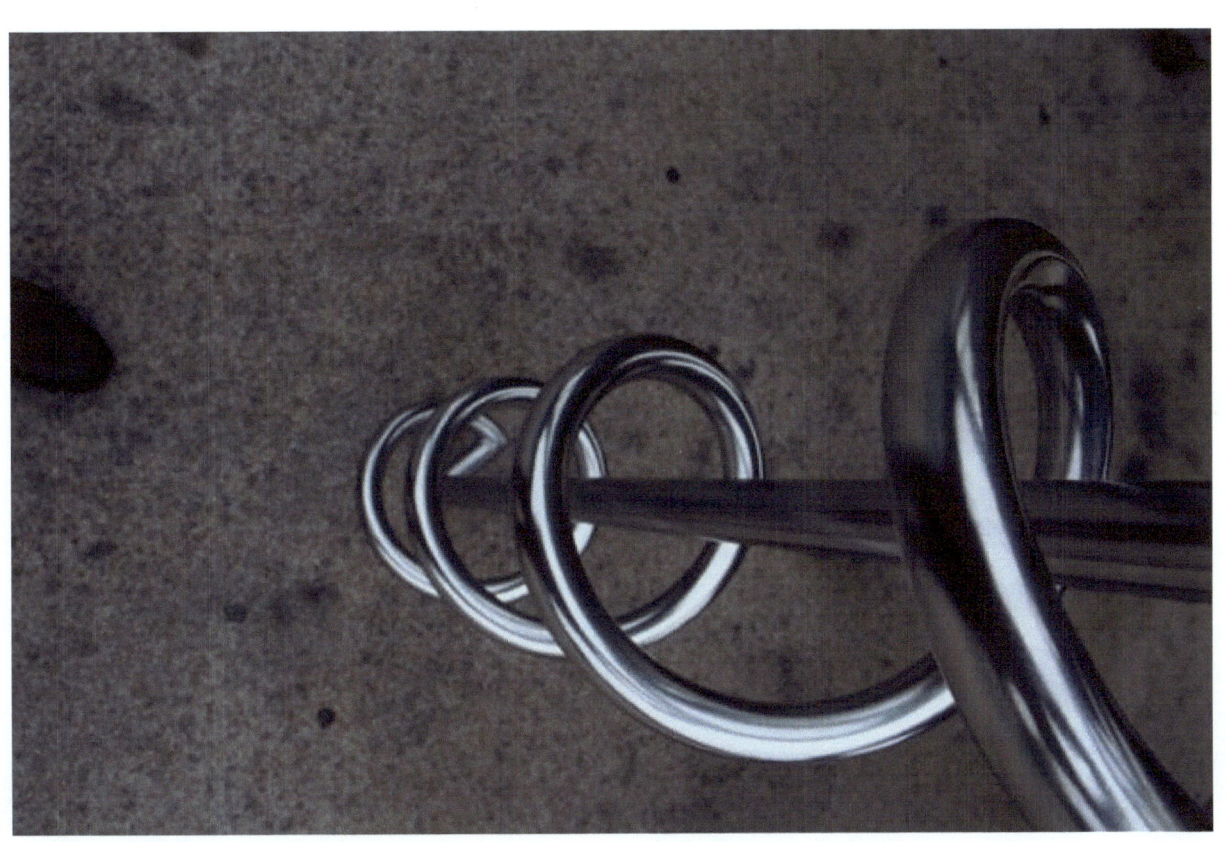

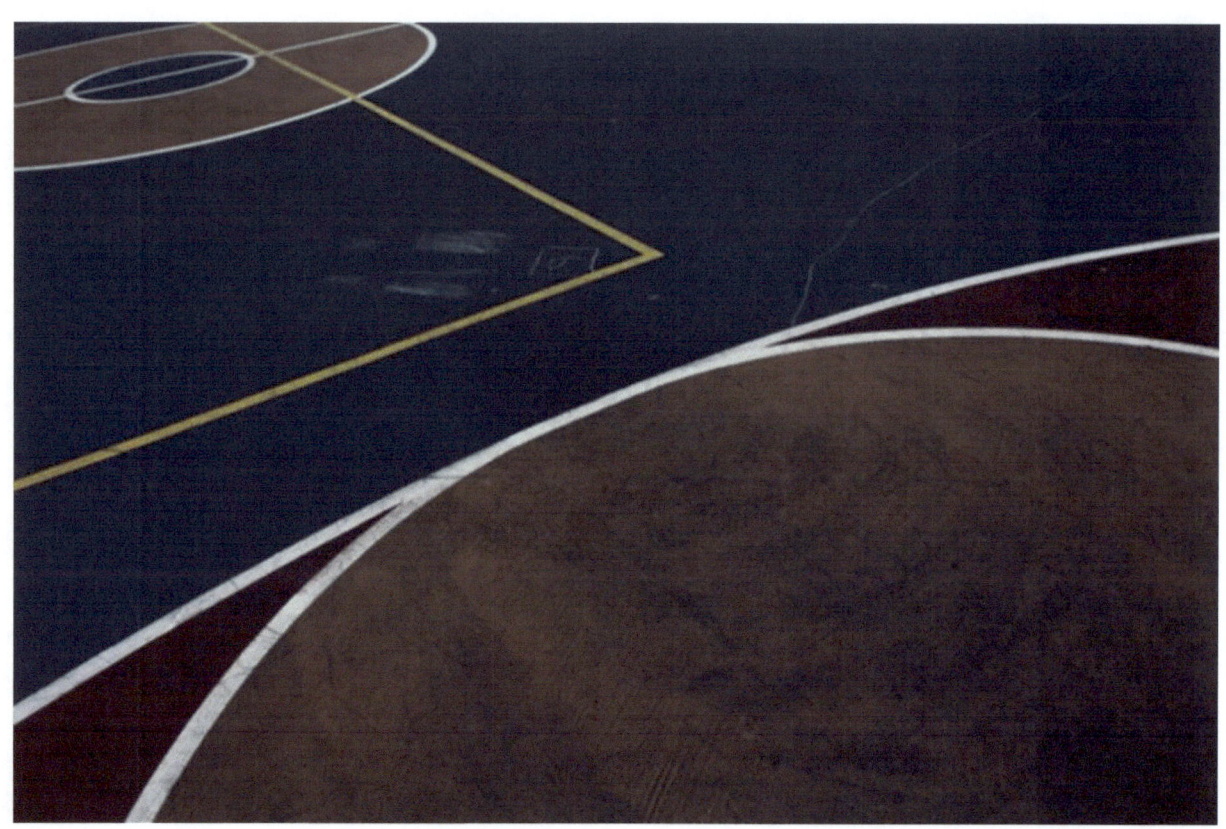

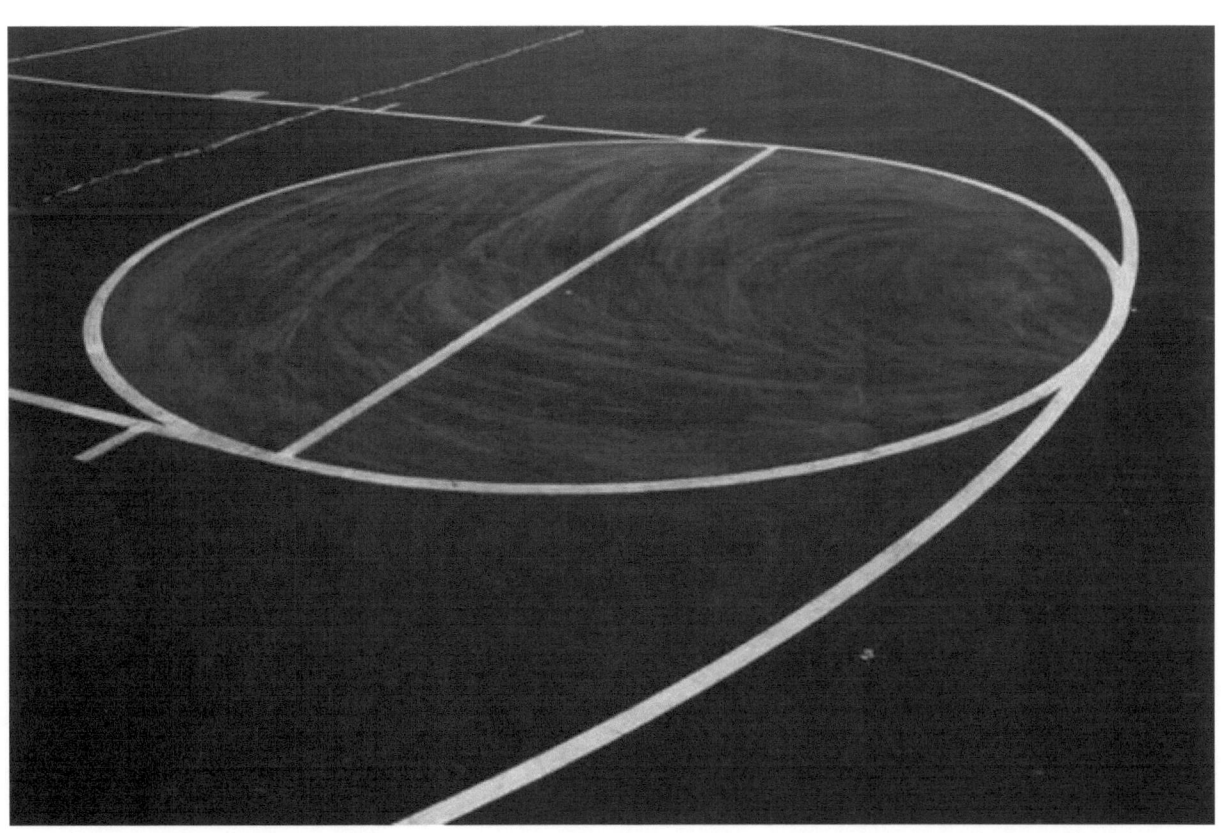

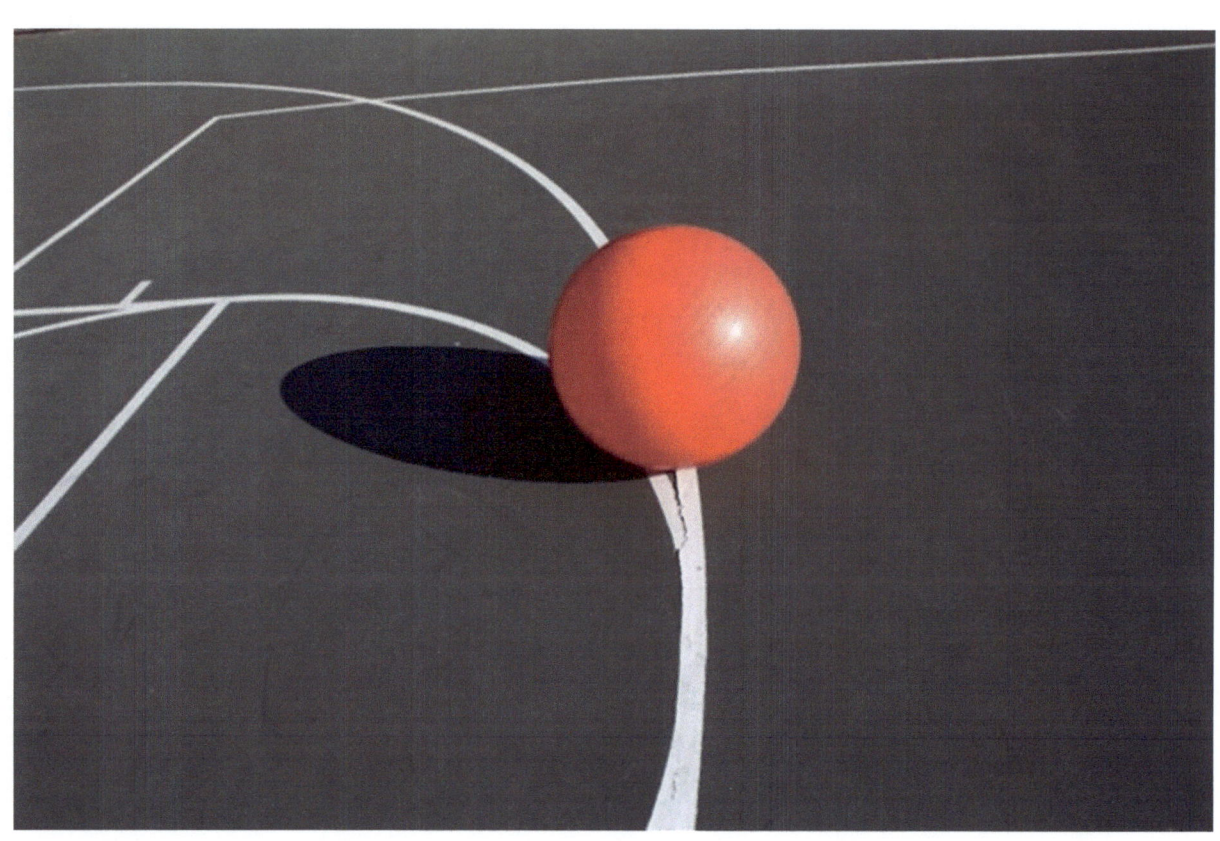

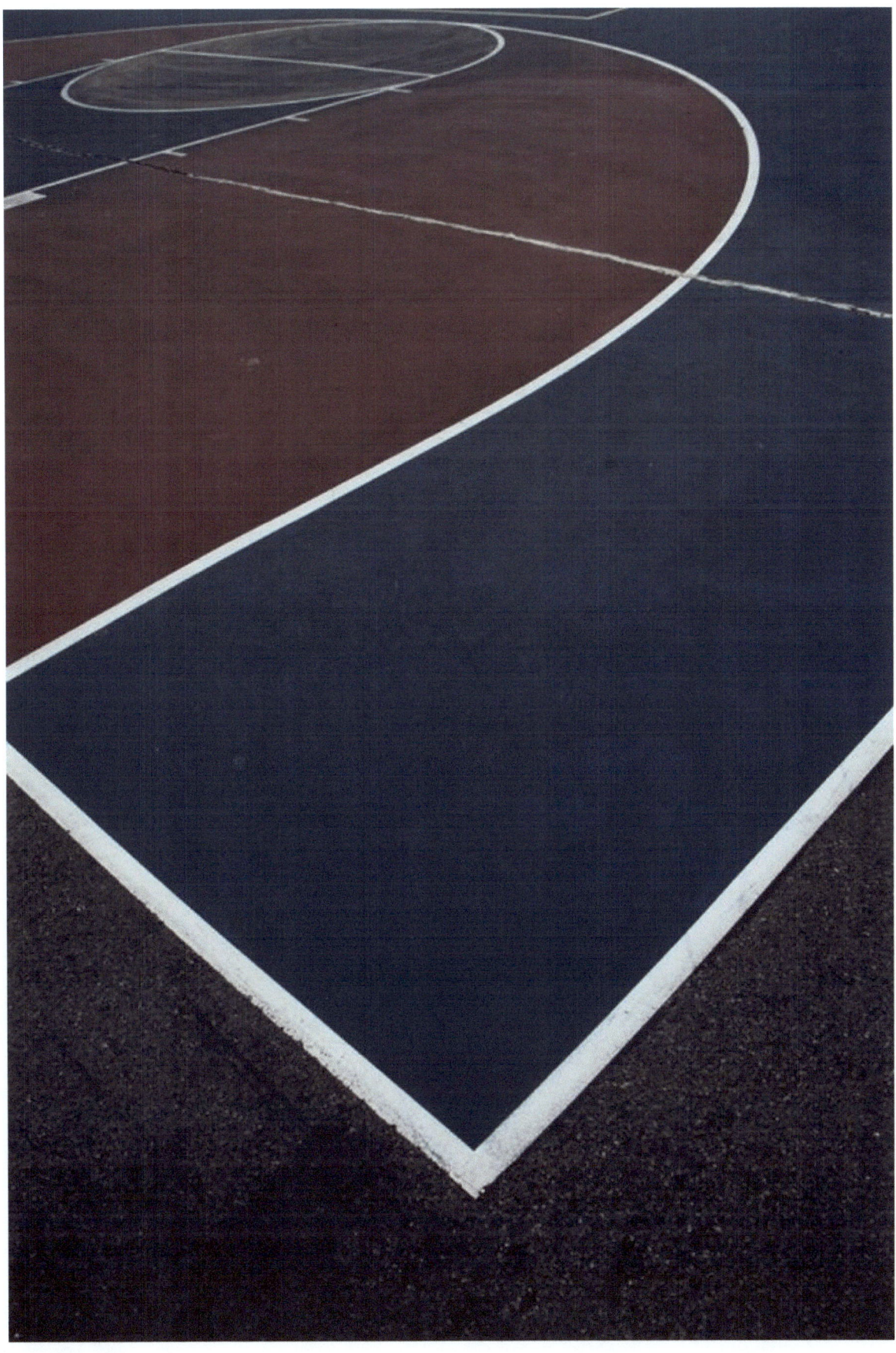

We see games as more than
lines and circles.
We see games,
we see events,
we see competitions.

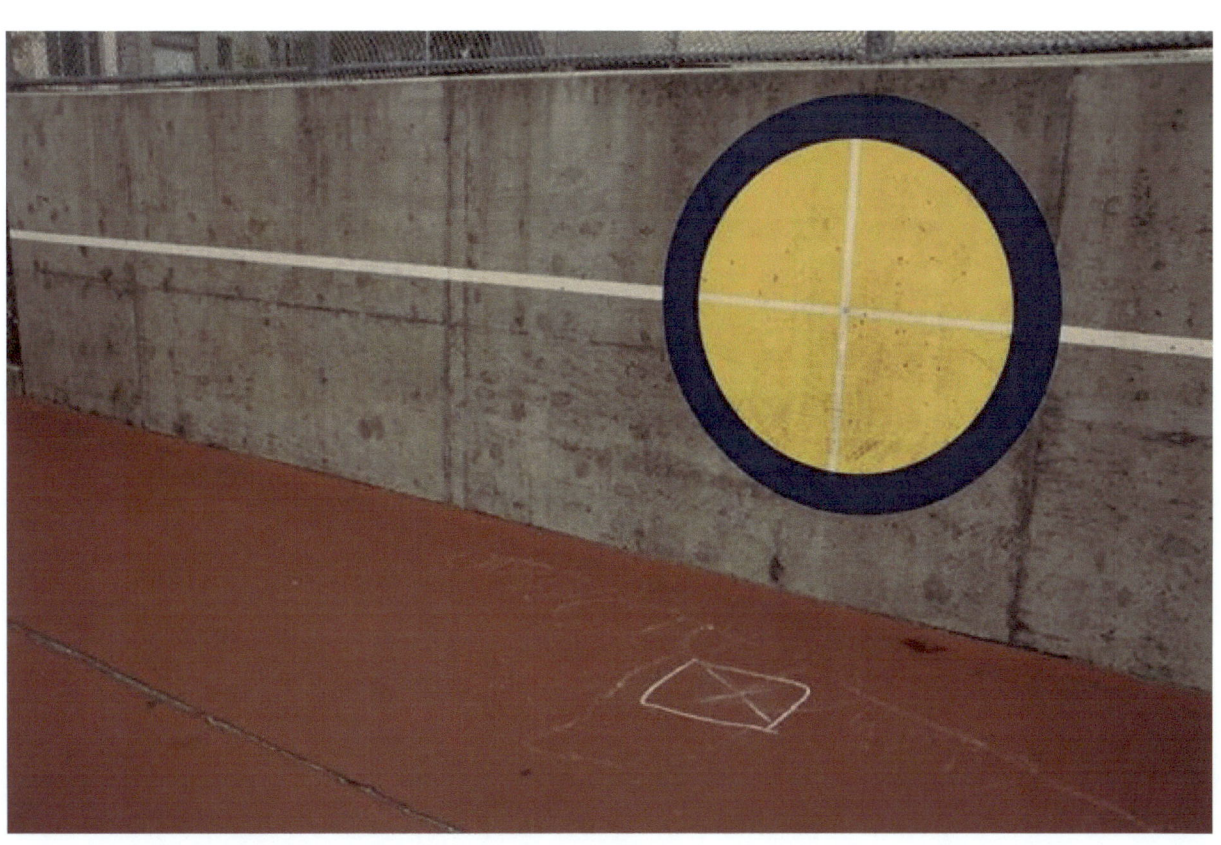

We see games.

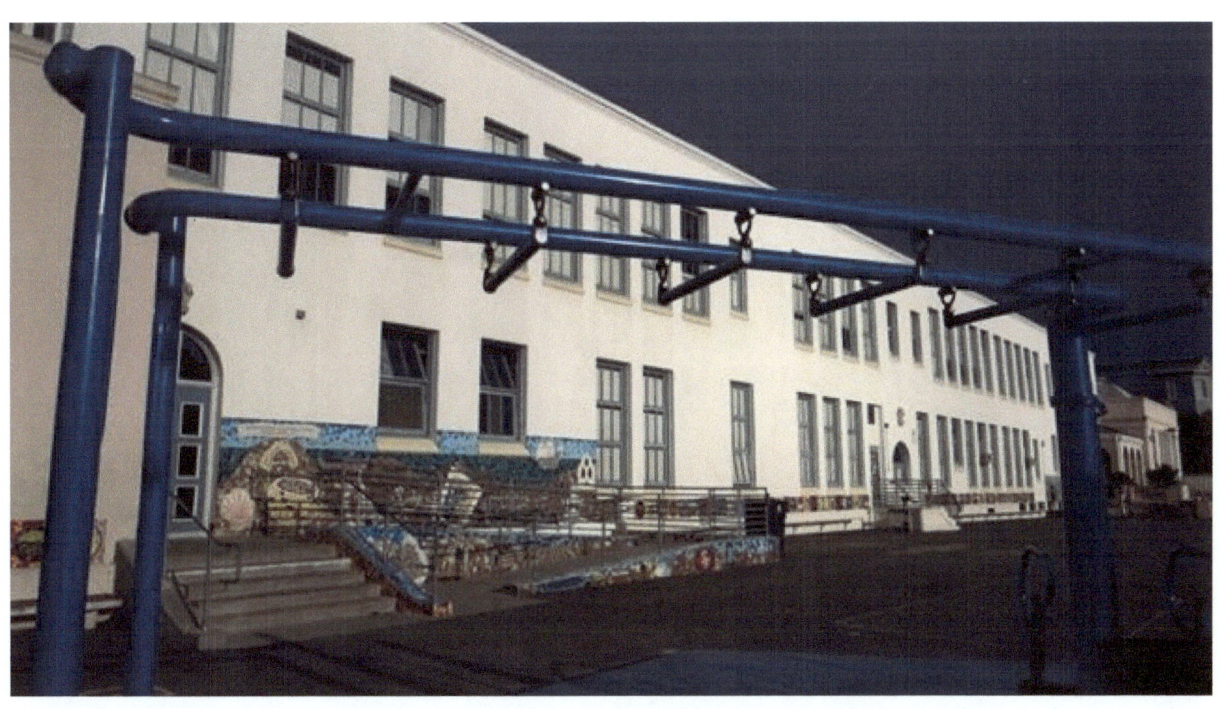

Finally, the play ground breaks out beyond
the bounds set for us in school.

We see lines as social interpretations:
Follow this line.
Stop at this spot.

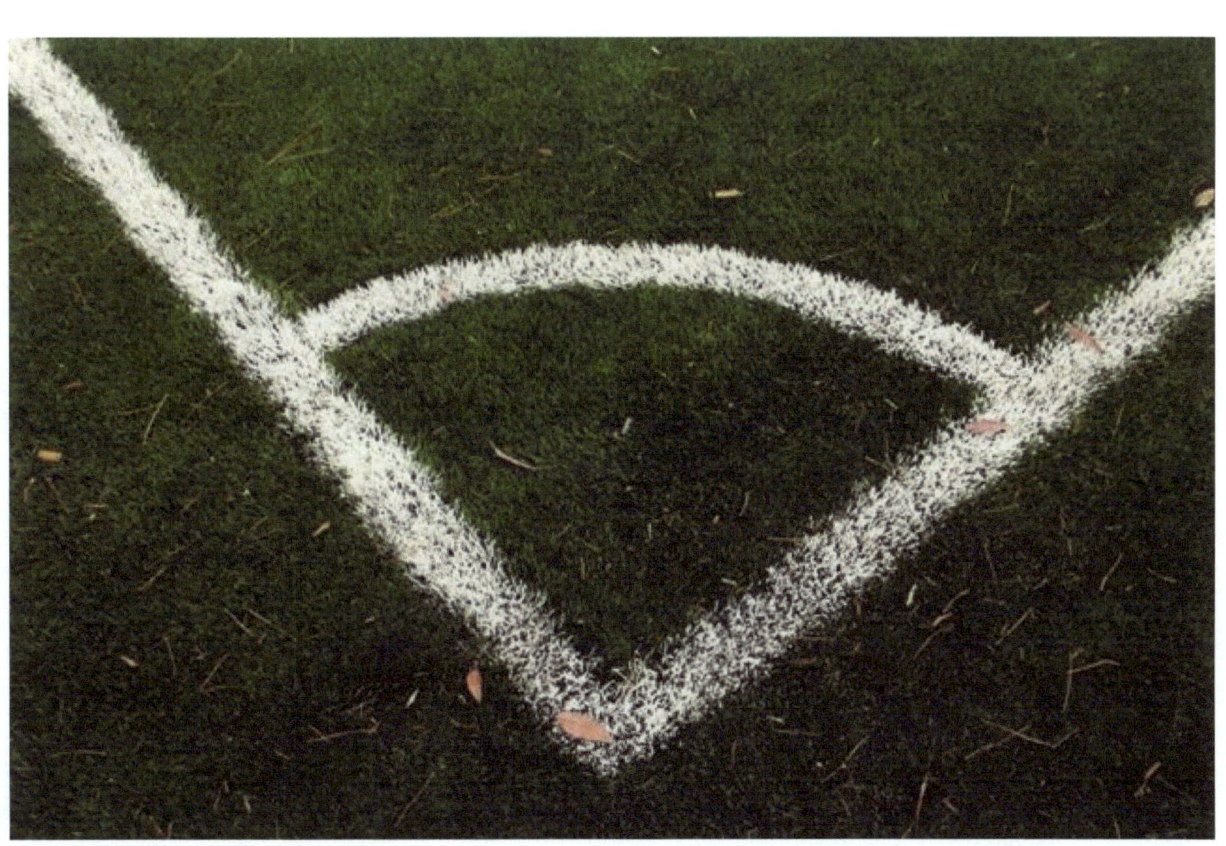

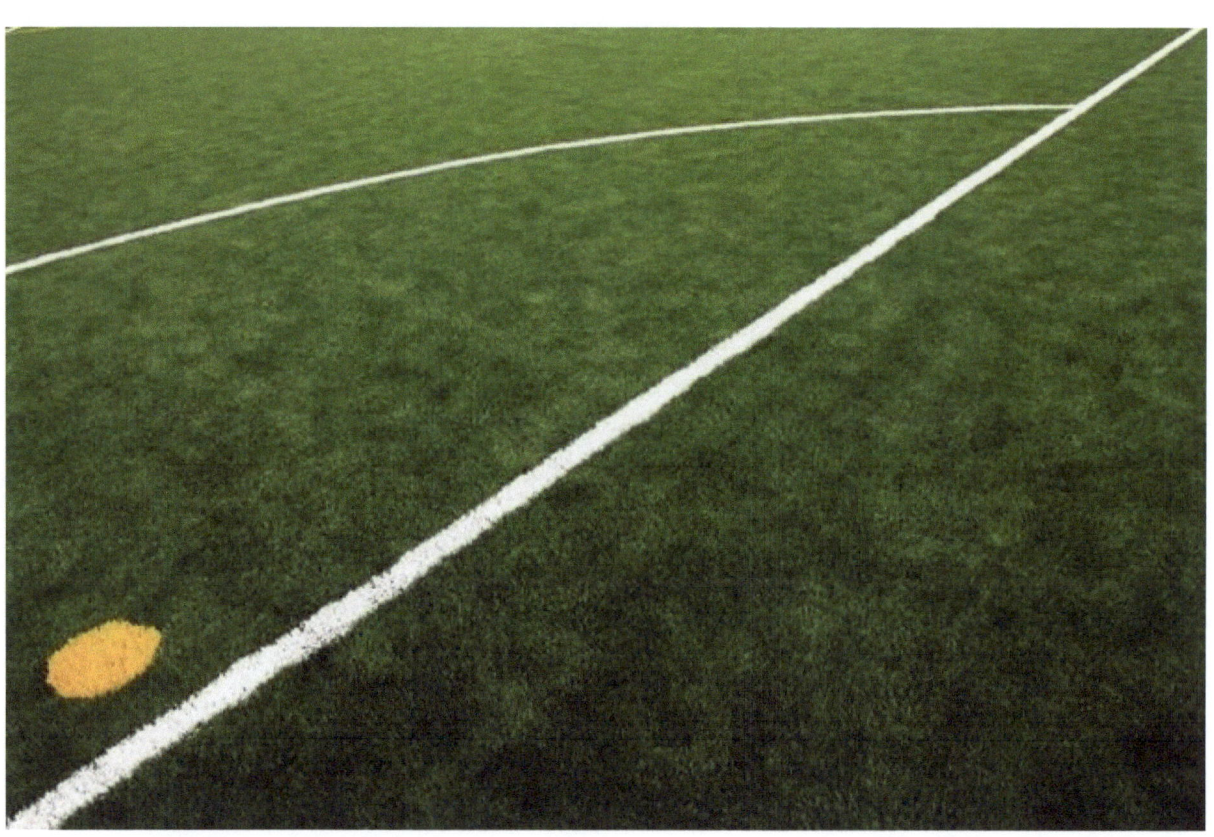

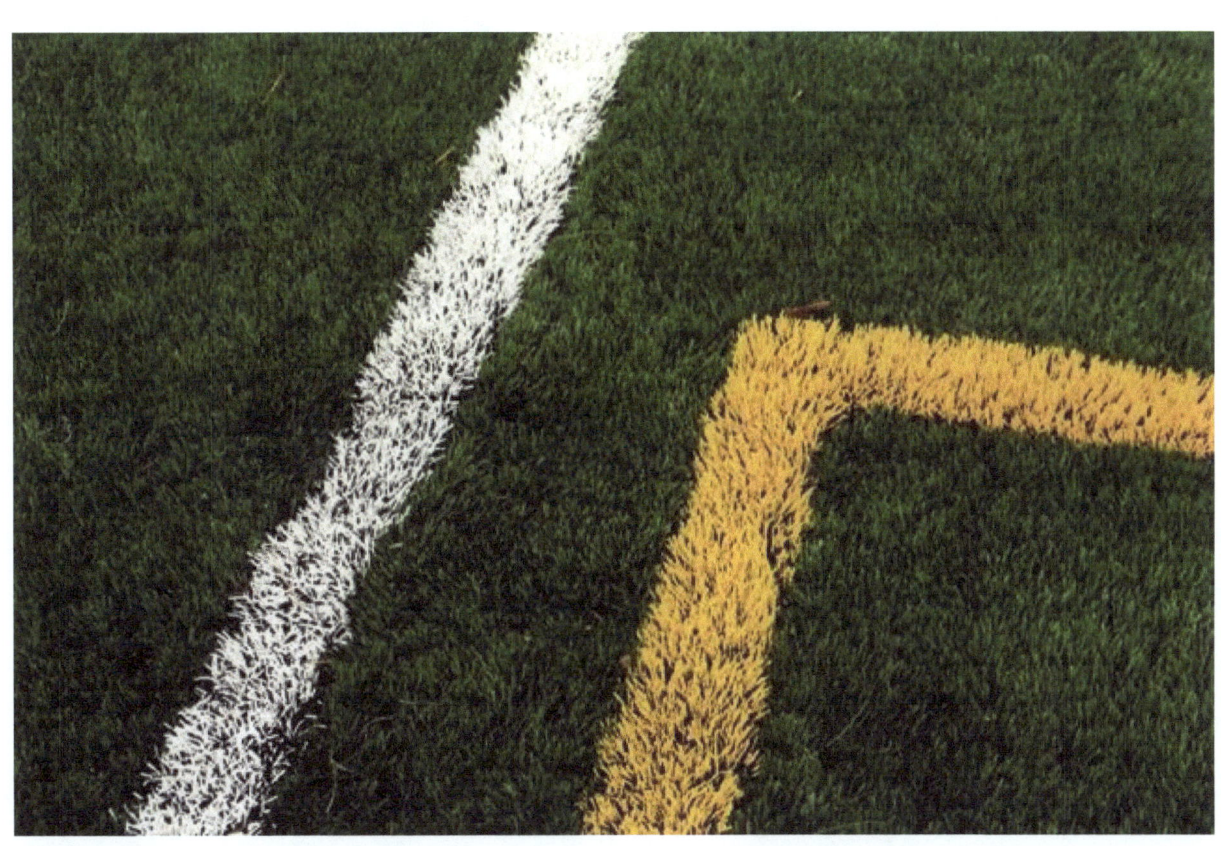

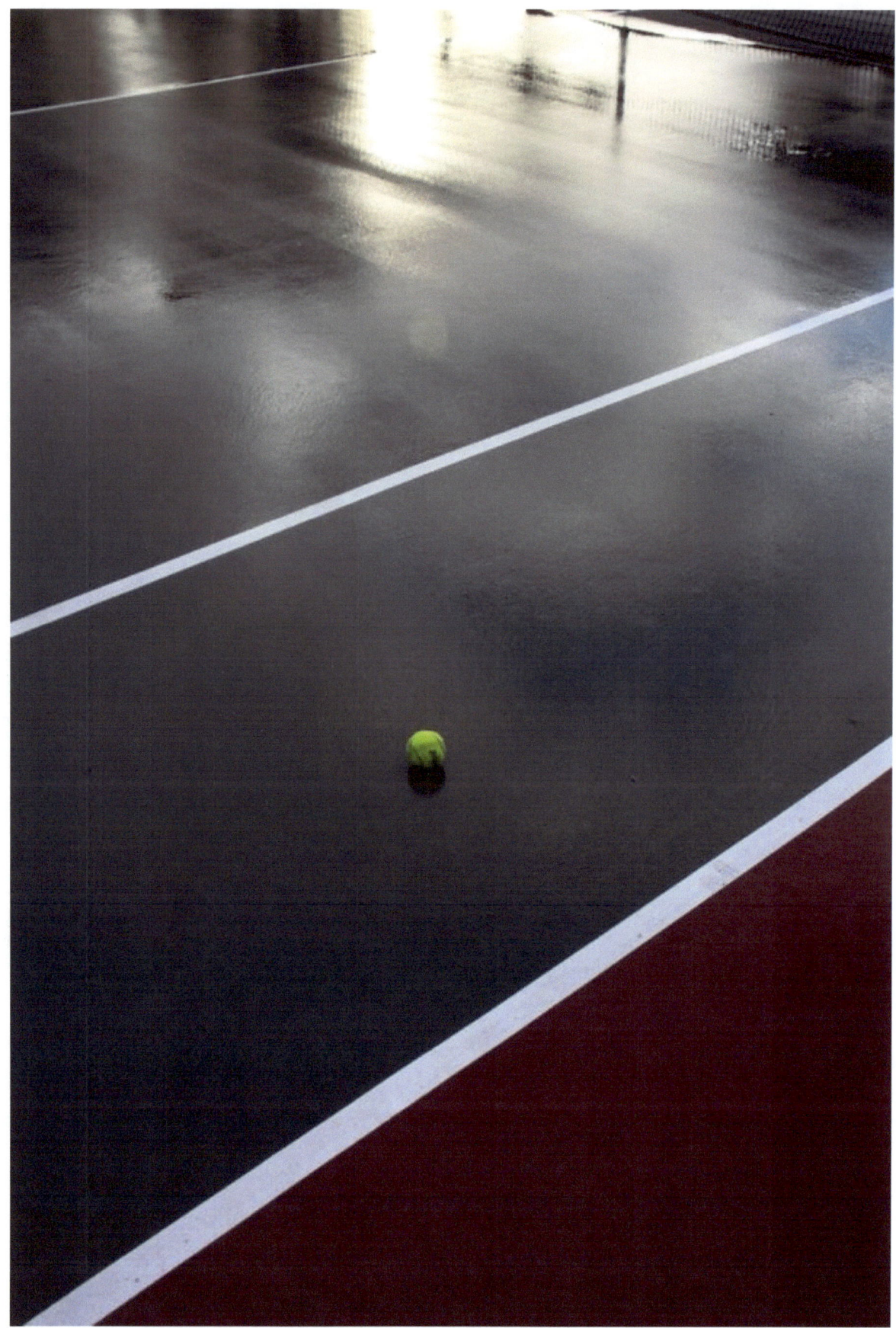

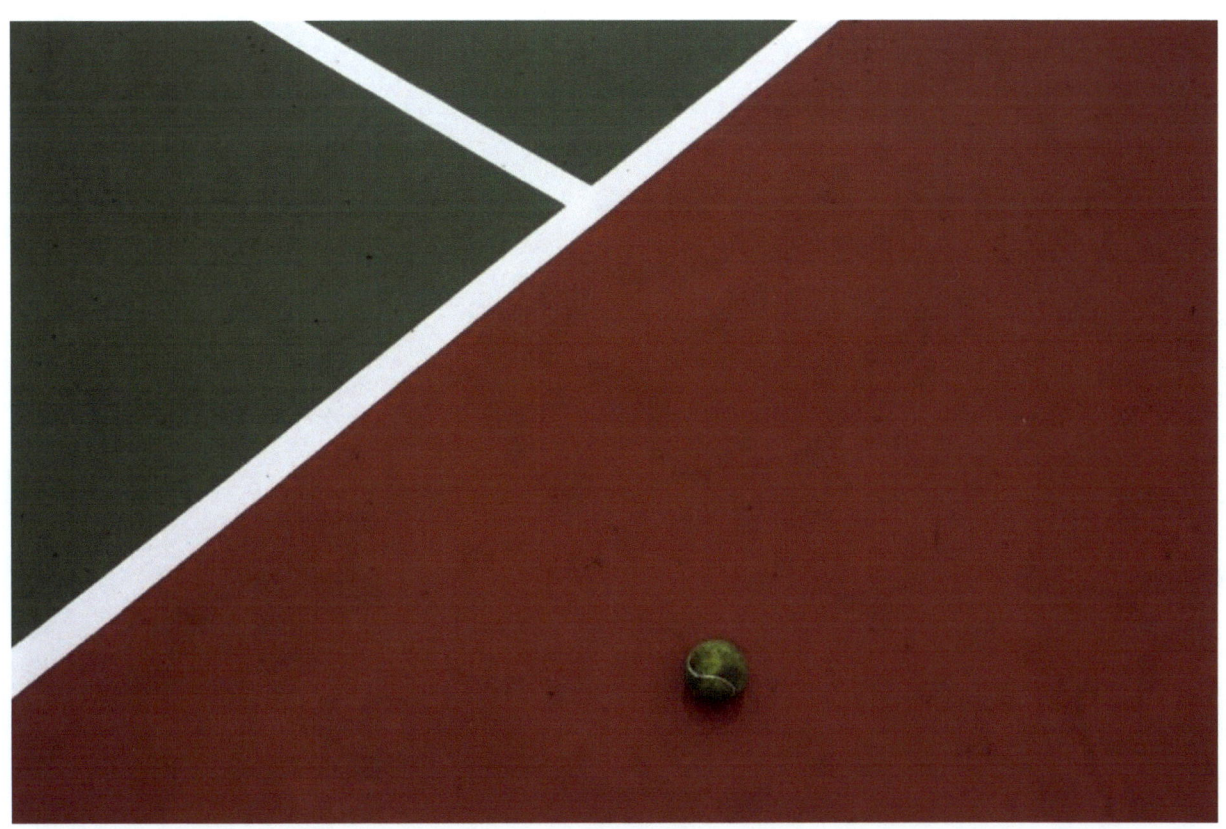

As we grow older,
the games on the play ground get more complex,
more involved.

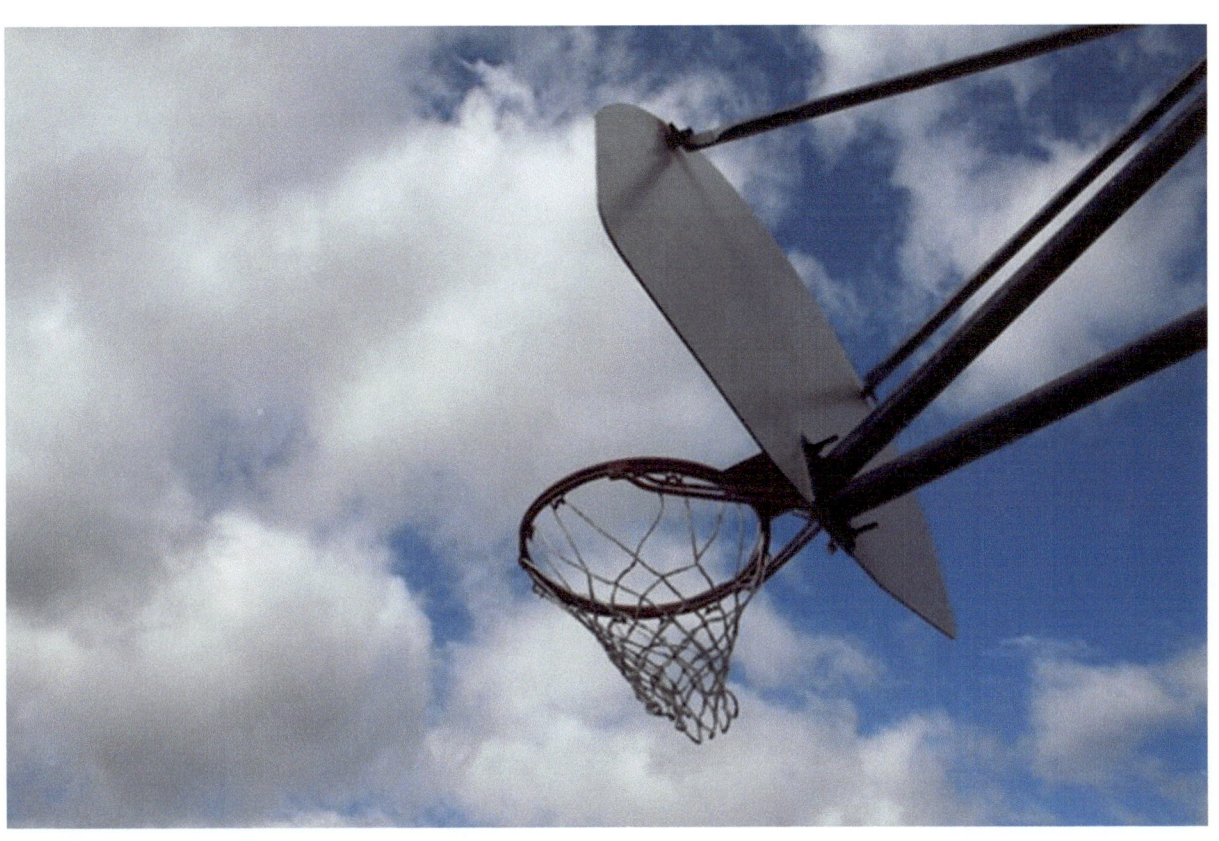

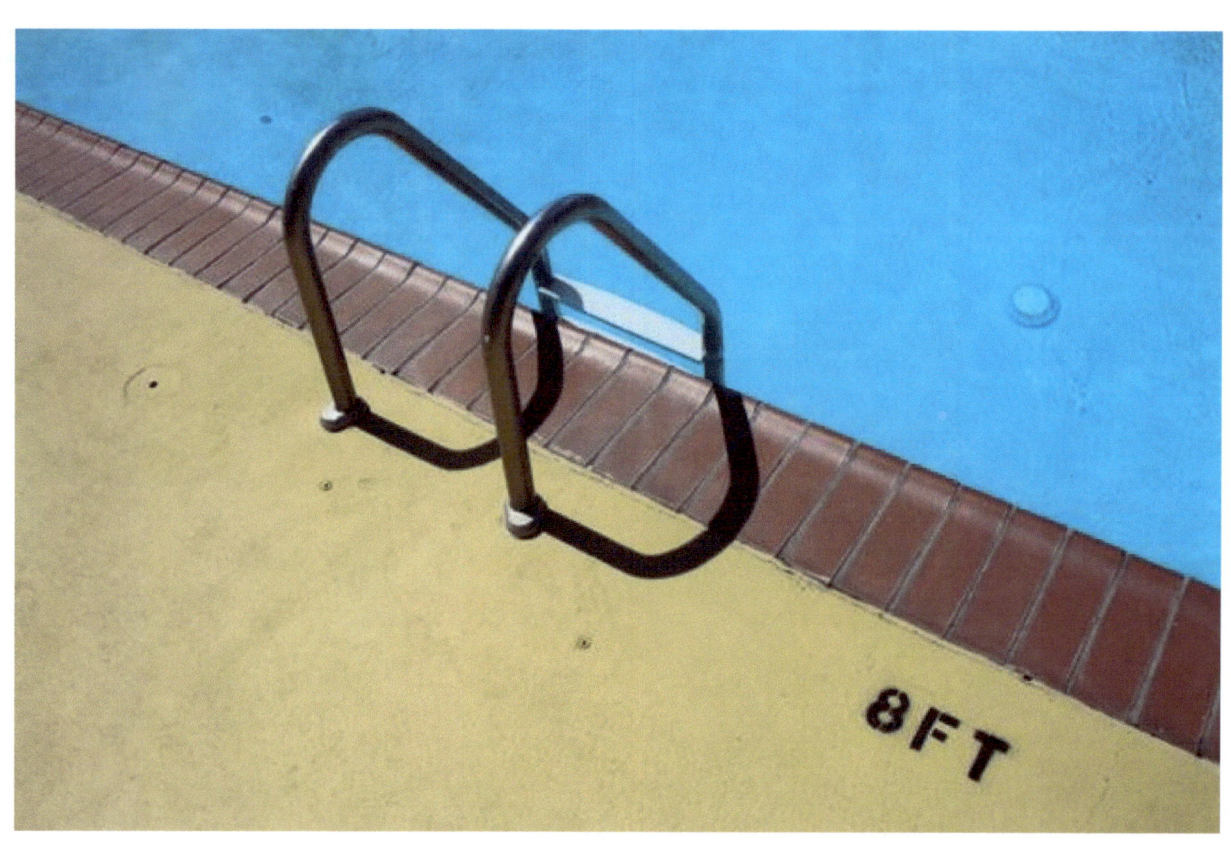

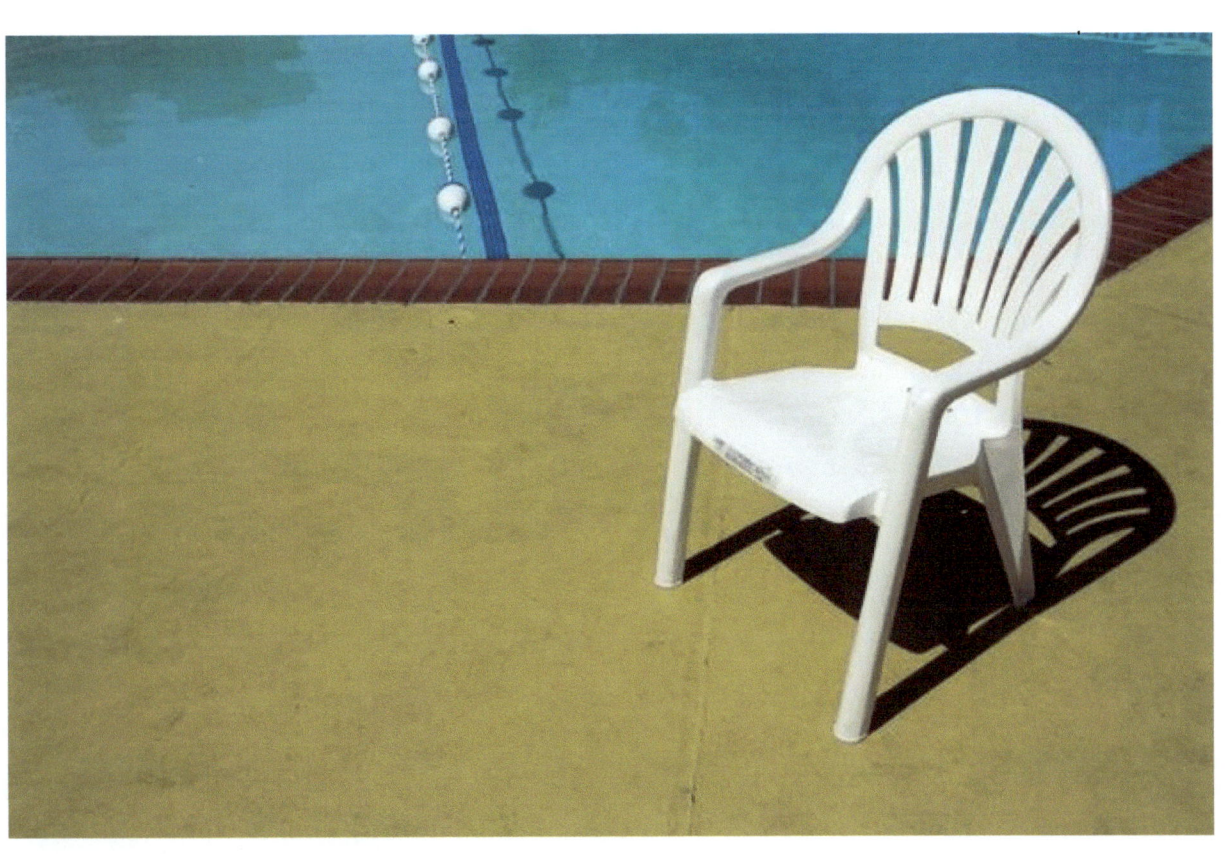

Sometimes we go off, beyond the play grounds, beyond the fields of play. We see how the culture intrudes on the greatest gift, the land, the streams, the cities.

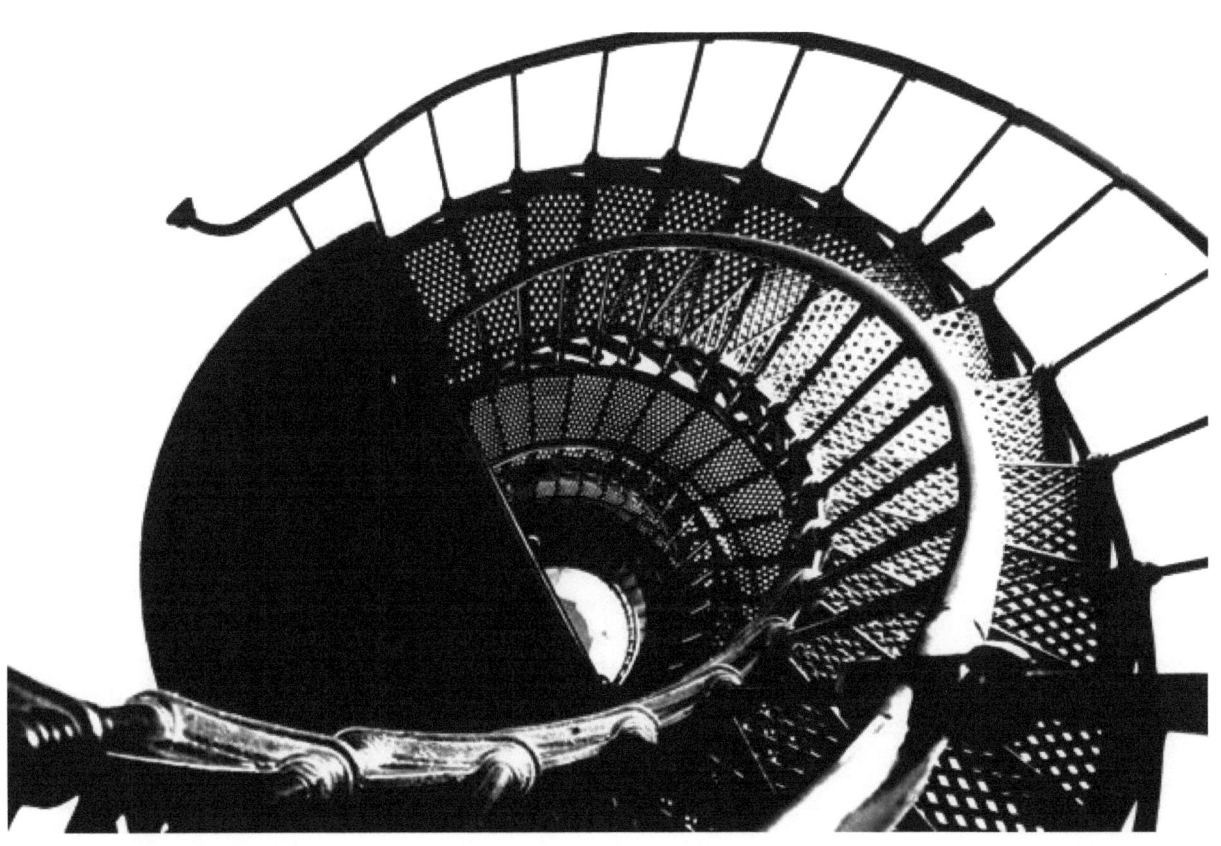

Is this a subject of being given life?

Or is it formed?
Starting with family
continuing through school
showing us how nature and society start out
interpreting for us.

Then, we interpret for ourselves.

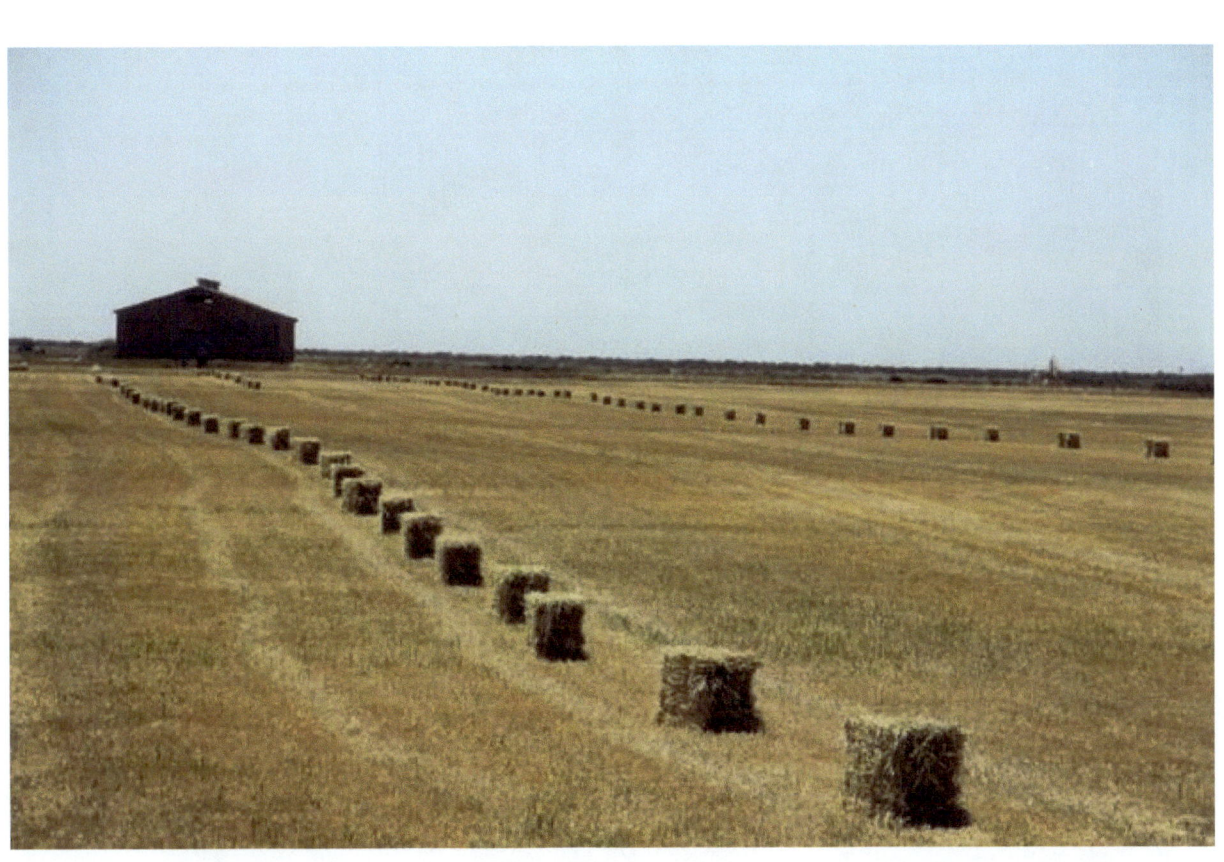

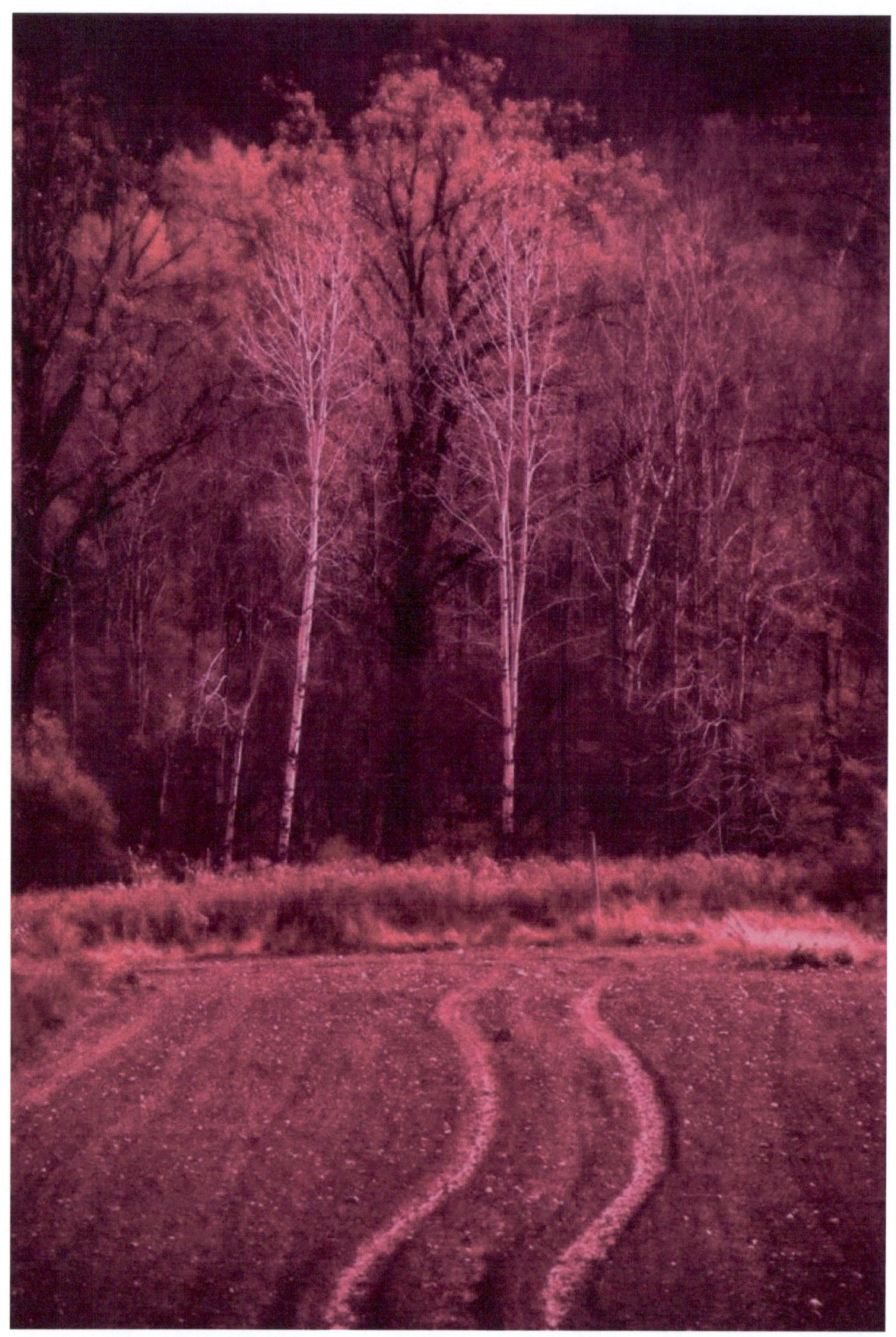

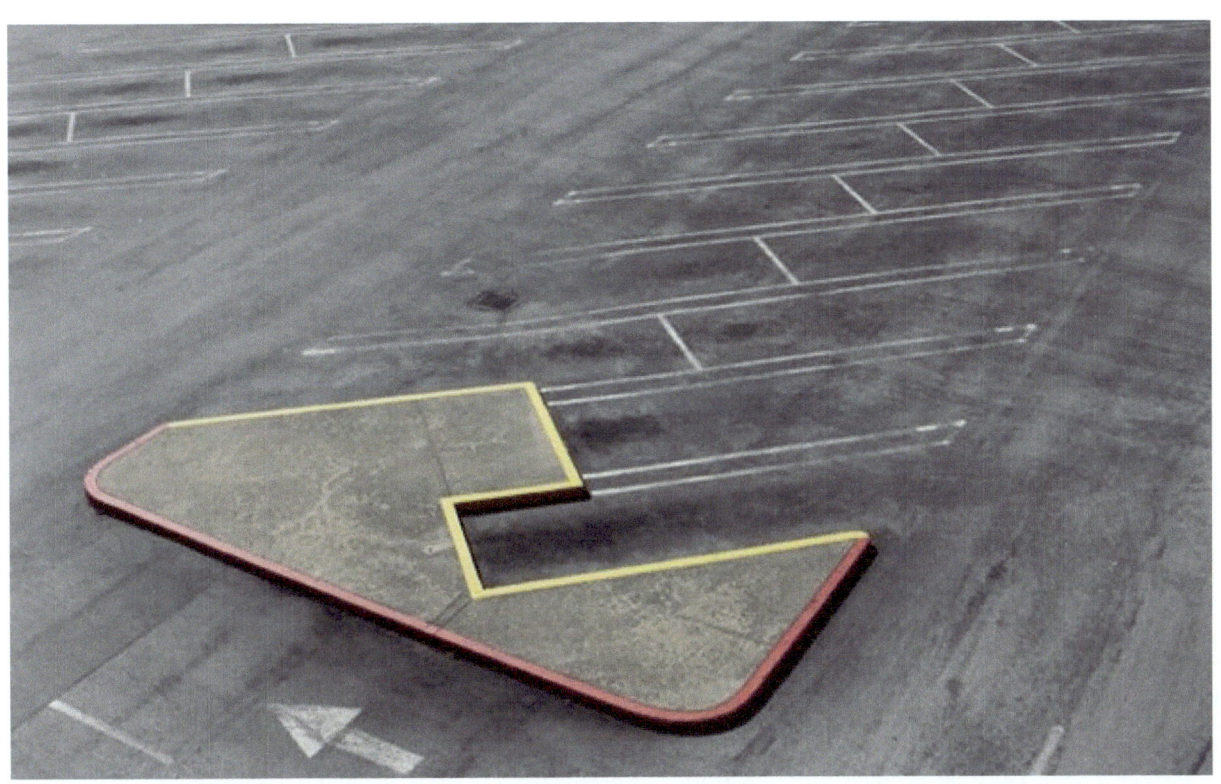

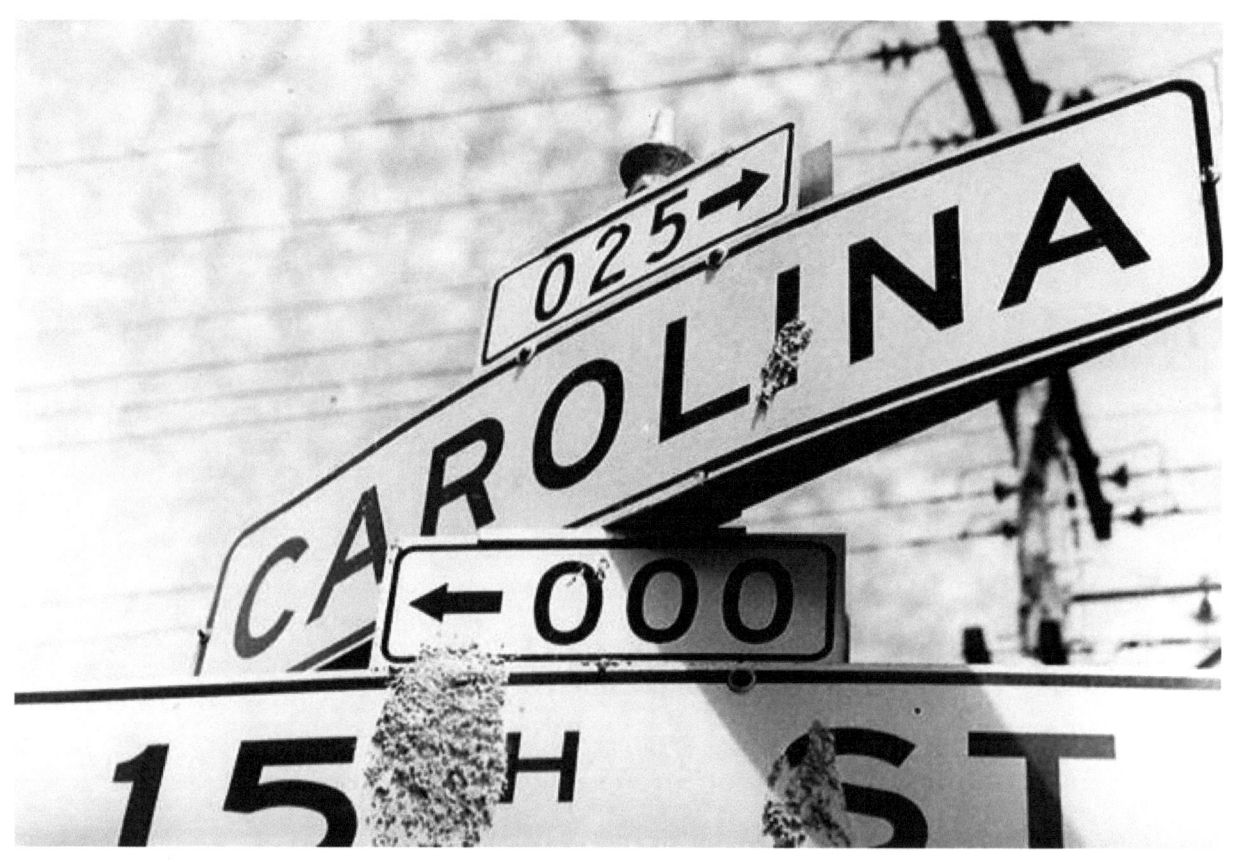

THIS PLAYGROUND IS DESIGNED TO SERVE CHILDREN BETWEEN THE AGES OF 5-12

PLAYGROUND IS CLOSED FROM DUSK TO DAWN

RULES OF THE PLAYGROUND

FOLLOW THE RULES - PLAY CAREFULLY

1. Do not use equipment without adult supervision
2. Do not use equipment when wet
3. Do not yell or scream
4. Wear proper footwear
5. No running, pushing or shoving
6. Do not use play equipment improperly
7. Do not bring any sharp objects such as glass, rocks, debris, etc.

The End

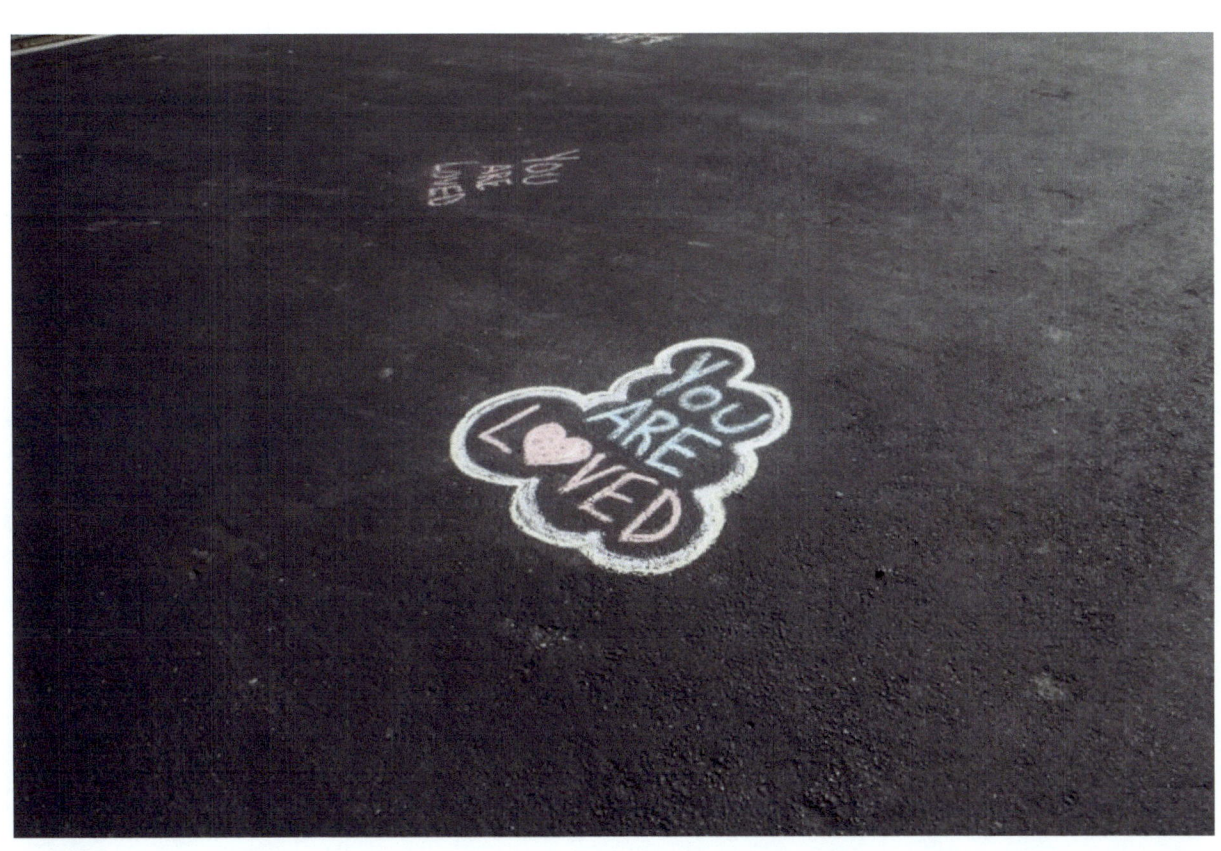